OU Women

Also available from Cassell:
P. Ainley: *Class and Skill: Changing Divisions of Knowledge and Labour*

Patricia W. Lunneborg

OU Women

Undoing Educational Obstacles

CASSELL

Cassell

Villiers House
41/47 Strand
London WC2N 5JE

387 Park Avenue South
New York
NY 10016–8810

British Library Cataloguing-in-Publication Data
A catalogue record for this book is available from the British Library.

ISBN 0–304–33161–9   (hardback)
      0–304–33163–5   (paperback)

Typeset by York House Typographic
Printed and bound in Great Britain by Redwood Books, Trowbridge, Wiltshire

Contents

Foreword

Few organizations have been transformed from an experiment into a national institution in so short a time. It is hard to believe that the Open University has existed for only twenty-five years. It is harder still to imagine how we did without it before it opened.

As a woman I take a vicarious pride in the fact that it was another woman politician, Jenny Lee, who was largely responsible for forcing through the idea of the Open University.

Now Patricia Lunneborg has written this thoroughly absorbing account of how the university has affected the lives of fourteen women. It is altogether appropriate that it should appear in the year of the Open University's silver jubilee.

I have a personal interest in the story of how these mature students obtained their bachelor's degrees. Their story could well have been my own. When I left school the opportunities for higher education were far fewer than they are today. In any case, I came from a working-class family. The lives of my mother and father had been dominated by unemployment and short-time working. There was no talk of sending me to university. The imperative was for me to start contributing to the household – if possible in a job which offered security and even a pension at the end of it.

So I can easily visualize myself as potential material for the Open University, with all the opportunities and challenges that would have involved. Instead, the life of politics intervened. But if this had not happened I am fairly certain that I, like the fourteen determined women in this book, and the many other OU students I have met up and down the country, would have been inspired to seek a degree.

Some two million people have studied with the university since it opened. We must congratulate all who have secured degrees in the past twenty-five years. But we should congratulate, too, those who did not manage to graduate. For them, surely, it was also worthwhile. I am convinced that all the students, even those who were gallant failures, must have had their lives enriched by the Open University, of which I am proud to be the new Chancellor.

Rt Hon. Betty Boothroyd MP, Speaker of the House of Commons

Acknowledgements

I am deeply indebted to Daphne Sarson, Administrative Officer of the Association of Open University Graduates (AOUG), for her help from the very beginning of the project. I am also indebted to Jean Posthuma, who lives in Wimbledon and organizes the London Open University Graduates Association. Both were invaluable in developing my interview questions. I also wish to thank the many women who responded to my articles in *Sesame* and *Omega*, indicating their willingness to participate. They were one source of interviewees, as were the lists of 1989–92 graduates who agreed to be contacted for publicity purposes, kindly supplied by Annette Mathias, OU Press Officer. I also greatly appreciated the encouragement of Giles Clark, OU Deputy Managing Editor, Book Trade.

But this book would never have seen the light of day without the support I received from the Women Writers Network and from Charlotte Oldfield and Tanja Howarth of the Tanja Howarth Literary Agency. Persistence is as vital to getting a book published as it is to getting a university degree, and it really helps to have other women saying, 'Persist, persist, persist, Pat.'

Preface

This book is about fourteen determined women. As you read through their lives, perhaps you'll respond: 'Right! My sister is a lot like Val who turned her life around. I bet if Sis read this, she might have a go at the Open University.' Or, 'It's not too late for my Mum! If Gertrude started at age 45, against all those odds, why couldn't Mum?' Or, 'What happened to Kushalta in school is just like what happened to me. I'll bet I can hold down my job and work on a degree, too, even if I haven't got any A-levels.'

This book is about women stirred up over higher education. It's about beating the system and beating the odds. It's about accepting the challenge that anyone, *anyone*, regardless of age and class and culture, who perseveres can get a university education. It's about people taking charge of their lives and writing new futures regardless of the past.

In January 1991 I, as an American observer, used the OU student paper, *Sesame*, and the graduates' newsletter, *Omega*, to ask about how the Open University had changed lives. I said that I wanted to talk with women from a wide variety of backgrounds in terms of age, class, race, culture, marital status, family finances, disabilities and occupations. What did the OU mean to them?

Responses came from everywhere. What diversity, what many-sidedness, there was to them! I was quite overwhelmed. I said to myself, what I'll have to do is simply choose somebody and start from there. Interview her, see what I've got, and then select another woman. Then I'll look at those two, and decide on the next.

Using Shirleen as an example, here's how I did it: Shirleen was born in South Africa, studied maths, and now is an actuary, a non-traditional career for women. She had been a housewife and did not work while doing the OU course. She is middle-aged, white, and missed a university education because her family could not afford it. After I had interviewed Shirleen, I said to myself, now I must make certain I interview women of colour, women employed outside the home continuously since school, women who are not married, women with traditional careers, and so on.

What we've got here, then, is a collage that represents the richness of returning learners' experiences and situations. I selected each woman so that she fitted like a piece into my evolving portrait and played as many roles – or covered as many bases, as we say in America – as possible.

I spent at least four hours with each woman and taped the interviews. I used to be a professor of psychology and women's studies, so I had an endless list of questions I wanted to explore. But these ten were the ones the women had the most to say about:

1. Why did you pursue an OU degree? What were your reasons?
2. What obstacles or constraints to study did you have?
3. What does the OU mean to you? How did it change your life?
4. What were the impacts of your OU degree on your career?
5. How might you see work or the notion of success differently now?
6. What is the most important use you make of your OU degree?
7. What were the hardest and easiest parts of OU study?
8. To what personal quality do you attribute your success at the OU?
9. What are your career plans?
10. What was most important in your life before and after the OU?

After I had transcribed the interviews and got everyone's story in the same order, I asked the Big Question that most writers answer at the start of a project. Aside from the fact that these women all did an OU degree, what do they have in common? What unites them? Is there a theme to their life stories?

It was right there in front of me. It wasn't their reasons for doing a degree. It wasn't the OU's impact on their careers. It was the obstacles they'd overcome, which, in themselves, were a surprise. I had expected present-day obstacles – money, husbands, job responsibilities. But they remembered school – long-ago humiliations, limited expectations and thwarted dreams. Hence, the subtitle: *Undoing Educational Obstacles*.

So, there are two kinds of chapter to this book, essays on those educational obstacles, followed by one or two of the women's stories to illustrate each point.

Chapter 1 is about how I got excited about the Open University and yearned to discover what had happened to the real women the play, and later the movie, *Educating Rita* was based on. Chapter 2, about Dale Godfrey, shows how, in spite of poverty and leaving school early because it literally made her sick, a young girl's aspirations can persist until they are achieved.

Classed schools are the topic of Chapter 3. Most UK schools are stamped 'middle-class' or 'working-class' depending on the social class of the majority of students. And who is least likely to go on to higher education? Working-class girls who go to working-class schools. Chapter 4 tells how Viv Steers overcame the results of a school that wouldn't let her do her A-levels in chemistry and physics because she was a girl, a school whose mission was to turn out clerks, not people who could go to university. Later Viv's OU degree gave her a second career, in midlife, in a foreign country.

Chapter 5, 'Streaming', is about sending youngsters to different school courses and different destinies depending on how well they do on examinations at age 11. Ability-streaming makes everyone who is not in the top stream feel an academic failure. Streaming for Pauline Swindells began in primary school, where the children who were thought capable of passing the 11-plus went into one class and the ones thought incapable went into another class, and the predictions became self-fulfilling. Chapter 7 tells how Ellen Davies failed the 11-plus but got into the grammar school the following year. Streamed into the arts, she couldn't take A-levels in the pure sciences and left at 16 to be a clerk. But the OU gave her the science courses she craved and the confidence to succeed at dental school.

Chapter 8, 'Channelling', attests to the continuing channelling of girls away from 'masculine' subjects both by society's notions of what subjects are appropriate for girls and, dismayingly, by sexist teachers. In spite of going to a good academic girls' school, Frances Smith, who begged to be a botanist, was repeatedly steered away from science and towards English, French and Latin. Finally, the OU released the real Frances, who feels she always was a natural scientist.

Early educational failure is the subject of Chapter 10. Failure has been called the 'English sickness' by Eric Bolton, renowned professor of education, and British schools 'succeed' in turning thousands of students off by making them feel like failures. Too many women leave school early, feeling that school is not a learning place. Misha Hebel fled the Isle of Sheppey after failing her A-levels, with the statutory five O-levels necessary for a civil service job. But with the mounting confidence she got from her OU studies, she adopted a new attitude: 'I will not be beaten.' Misha no longer has the 'English sickness'.

Chapter 12, on low self-confidence, confirms two things: why girls do better in single-sex than mixed-sex schools, and why later in life, women returners, more than men returners, have low academic self-confidence, especially if they've been at home with children. Chapter 13 is the story of Kushalta Saini, the only child of a couple from North India. As such, she felt enormous pressure to do well in school and not let the family down. Failing O-levels the first time and having a difficult time studying for A-levels lowered her shaky self-esteem even further. The OU gave Kush a way to succeed brilliantly in two areas at once, at work and at school.

Male bias is the focus of Chapter 14. Why in mixed-sex schools do boys get more attention from their teachers than girls? Why do teachers let boys dominate classroom activities? Small wonder girls do better in girls-only schools, where they get better exam results and are more likely to want and expect that they will go on to higher education. The story of Teresa Davis (Chapter 15) illustrates how male bias can begin at home. Teresa, a would-be doctor, watched her brother go to Eton and have tutors and receive the education she desired. She, instead, went to boarding schools geared towards the arts. How could she hope to succeed at A-levels in physics, chemistry and biology? Through the OU, she got her science degree and, while not a physician, works right next to them at Guy's Hospital in London.

Chapter 16, on lack of emotional support, documents the need of women to have their families of origin, and the families they create, lend them emotional support in their quest for an education. One of the most important things teachers can do is to get parents to back their daughters' aspirations. Helen Seddon, in Chapter 17, says, 'I don't believe anybody had any expectations of me. I don't think my parents expected me to be any good at anything. So I didn't have any great expectations of myself.' Passing her first OU course gave her the inner strength to believe what no one else had, that she could succeed, so thereafter she did.

Lack of financial support is tackled in Chapter 18. Families are probably more equitable about financing daughters' educations today, but today's government isn't as generous where women returners are concerned. As Tessa Blackstone says, 'However poor a part-time student is, he or she has to pay. Clearly this is inequitable.' Who better to tell women how to hold down a full-time job, raise a family and pay for their own college education than Editha Tharpe, who in Chapter 19 relates the kinds of non-support British women get from their employers.

Chapter 20 documents university life's lack of fit with the realities of women's lives – why a mature woman with a family and job has small hope of success doing a conventional degree at a traditional university. Shirleen Stibbe, of Chapter 21, is not a house-proud homemaker, but she is a devoted mother. How else but through the OU could she be there for her boys at the end of their school day *and* do an honours degree in maths?

Gertrude Mtandabari, the OU graduate of Chapter 22, also wanted to be there for her boys while she got a college degree and held down a full-time job. But there were other reasons why a traditional university was difficult for Gertrude to contemplate. Not only is Gertrude's native tongue German, but she is deaf in one ear.

The last obstacle to women's higher education is briefly considered in Chapter 23. Men are not, but women are, socialized for the homemaker role. We all know that men should be taking care of home and children too, but actions are slow to follow beliefs. To illustrate our socialization I have chosen two women. Janaki Mahendran (in Chapter 24) tells us of her early education in Sri Lanka and her frustrated desire to become a doctor. Today in London, she cares for an extended family while her physician husband provides the financial wherewithal. Armed with her OU degree, she is now an expert on resolving problems in human interaction.

Val Burke was content to raise two daughters after she flunked out of university – except that she really wasn't satisfied. Chapter 25 tells how the OU let her be both a homebody and a scholar, and do a degree she never dreamed she was capable of – computer science.

Chapter 26, 'The OU: Undoing Educational Obstacles', sums up both what the Open University is like and the major lessons the experience of these women offers for returners.

Following the References is a list of Selected Resources to get mature women started on the road to further and higher education.

Chapter 1

Introduction

Until three years ago, Victoria and Lucy were close friends. But today they feel they have little in common. Victoria's parents sent her to an all-girls private school, Lucy's to the local, mixed, state secondary school. Despite their childhood friendship, they view each other warily from opposite sides of the educational divide . . . 'The school is narrow, and that has made me more conscious of social class. In the past, if I met someone new I'd just accept them. Now I examine every word. A certain accent would be a real setback. And clothes too.' These days, when Lucy and Victoria meet, they find little to talk about. Lucy thinks girls at Victoria's school look down on her and her friends. Victoria says she feels very different from her old schoolfriends: 'It's funny but I'm quite sure that if Lucy had come to my school, she'd be just like me.' (Buxton, 1993)

What do we Americans know about British education? Precious little. Unless we have a professional interest in it, we form our ideas principally from movies, Masterpiece Theatre and *Time* magazine.

Here's what my American background taught me. From *Brideshead Revisited* and *The Prime of Miss Jean Brody* I learned that the British upper classes are taught by governesses and tutors, or they go to girls' and boys' boarding schools at a very tender age, or they attend local, what we would call 'private', schools. Then at about age 18 the boys go to Oxford or Cambridge, and the girls . . . Ah, what happens next to the girls isn't as clear. Don't most get married as soon as they find a good match?

To Sir with Love broadened my perspective. I learned that England also has tough inner-city kids totally turned off by school. Just as in America, they hate it and can hardly wait to be old enough to leave and get a job. But in England, sensitive, caring, determined teachers *save* them, girls and boys alike. Thanks to Sidney Poitier, Lulu had a future. I wasn't sure she could get into Oxford, but she had learned to like learning.

What happens to ordinary people in between the rich and poor within the British educational system doesn't seem to be the stuff of movies and magazine articles, so I remained in the dark where ordinary people were concerned. But thanks to *Time*, *People* and *Newsweek* magazines, I kept up with how royal youth were faring. In contrast to the Princes who went to Oxford or Cambridge if they were so inclined, Princess Diana had left school without any qualifications. Like most Americans, I felt that was a shame. It sure looked like the system had failed her – a princess!

I also learned that Di did have a chance, a second chance. Everybody in the UK had a second chance. That's what *Educating Rita* was all about. Even if you had an inebriated Michael Caine as your unreliable tutor, if you worked very hard, if you ignored your unsupportive relatives, and if you hung out with your new student peers, you could get a college education. Starting at Ground Zero, you could enroll in something called the Open University and get a bachelor's degree. Wow!

Imagine my delight when in 1989 my husband Cliff began writing text material with the statistics faculty at the Open University's 'campus' in Milton Keynes. This campus is even weirder than Milton Keynes itself, which looks like it belongs in the American heartland. This college campus has no students!

On my first visit to the OU I headed straight for the library. I wanted to read more about Rita and her friends. I was looking for a book that would tell me what sort of women signed up with the OU and what happened to them. *Why* did they do the OU course? *How* did they manage, with job and family responsibilities? *What* obstacles did they overcome to make it? And what happened *when* they had their degrees? Did the OU change their lives?

Well, I couldn't find such a book – which is why I put this one together. How can I say I wrote it? Fourteen other women wrote it. I've simply tried to organize the results.

How to bind their stories together with a theme remained a mystery until I had finished interviewing, transcribing and getting my tapes into some kind of order. Then, there it was in front of me – the question about obstacles. What I had expected in the way of answers was lack of money, unhelpful husbands and no room of their own. What I got instead were memories. Unhappy memories of education many years ago. Unsupportive parents, brothers being favoured, failed exams, schools lacking expectations of their students.

I wrote down the ten chief barriers to education that the women gave me and started reading for evidence that . . . what did I expect? I expected to read that these barriers, indeed, had existed, but today were no more. I found, sadly, that the obstacles are very much in place.

Nonetheless, I devote a minimal amount of space to the negative – the barriers within the system – and a maximum amount of space to the women's lives – which are forward-looking, upbeat, moving ahead from one challenge to another, and succeeding.

And if streaming and channelling and male bias and society's primary socialization of women as homemakers are still with us, so too is the Open University! And it continues to be one of the best ways for women to beat the system.

Here, then, are Dale, Viv, Pauline, Ellen, Frances, Misha, Kushalta, Teresa, Helen, Editha, Shirleen, Gertrude, Janaki and Val. Seven of them wrote to me after seeing my appeal in the OU student newspaper. Seven I sought out from lists of graduates willing to talk about their lives. More details about mature students and the OU are found in the last chapter.

Which woman came the farthest in terms of overcoming obstacles? That's unanswerable; or the answer is *all* of them. But I had to choose one to start us off, and it is Dale Godfrey. Dale grew up in a fatherless home in Dundee, where her mother chose to be poor and employed, rather than poor and on social security. Her mum worked long days in factories and her grandmother did cleaning jobs and was a home worker, sewing labels on clothes. All Dale's friends' mothers worked as well. Her mother faced the choice for Dale between a middle-class grammar school and a highly touted new comprehensive in a lower-class catchment area, a decision which profoundly shaped Dale's life.

Chapter 2

Dale Godfrey   *From Volunteer to Fundraising Manager*

I'd got the *Guardian* to read on the train and I was thinking, what do I want to do after this year? I'd read an advert and think, Oh, that's a nice job. And then I'd reject it because . . . long hours, lots of travelling, not enough flexibility, wrong part of the country, wrong for the family. I was still thinking back to children this age [she points to a photo of two little girls]. I don't know if there'll ever be a time when I'd move away from home to work during the week, but then again, why not? Why not, if it was the ideal job for me and it was all right with us as a couple? Why be thinking family things, when I can do anything?

Dale Godfrey's house in Wootten Bridge on the Isle of Wight was a cab ride from the ferry dock, and the whole way our pony-tailed cabbie complained to Cliff and me that tourism was dead. He was leaving, he groused, because families could fly to Florida now for a cheaper holiday than they'd get on the Isle of Wight. He'd drive a cab somewhere else. Dale and David Godfrey will leave the Isle some day as well, and probably it will also be because of career considerations.

Dale, dressed in slacks and sweater and wellingtons, came to the door with Amber, her golden retriever, in tow. She is a tall, slender, pale woman with a mass of curly dark-brown hair and laughing eyes. Cliff went off shivering into the biting January air with an Ordnance Survey map. Amber went off grumbling to her big bed in the hall, and Dale and I settled down with coffee and biscuits. Two picture windows met in the corner behind Dale's head, with a view of bare trees and blue skies. Her shrubbery housed several bird families that trilled happily the whole day.

This is what Dale had written in January 1991:

I am now forty. I started with the OU ten years ago having left school at the age of fifteen with no formal qualifications. Three years into my OU degree, I moved with my family – I am married and have two teenage children – to the Isle of Wight. Within a few weeks, I was approached to 'fill in' teaching GCE Psychology at the local college. The initial few hours a week led to in-service teacher training. Meanwhile, I continued with the OU degree and graduated in 1986, then continuing for Honours. Two years ago I replied to an advertisement for a researcher with a national charity, the Royal National Institute for the Deaf (RNID). I was successful and am carrying out an extensive study on the island. A recent development of this is the employment of three other staff. I am currently on a management course and am involved in the organization regionally and nationally as well as on a local level. The OU has given me a lot in all sorts of ways. I can't think of any other institution which could have given me such a wide range of experiences and opportunities.

Why did you pursue an OU degree?

I wanted a degree, but the way I described it to other people and also to myself was much more defensive than that. My first year I was thinking, if I do this first year, I will be satisfied. That will be enough. I was thinking of a teaching career, but if I had really wanted to be a teacher, the local teacher training college was recruiting mature women without even O-levels. So what I wanted was to stretch myself.

What obstacles to succeeding at the OU did you have?

When I left school at 15 it was because I was very, very unhappy. My father died in 1953 so I lived with my mother and grandmother. My early education was at a local primary school on Dundee's outskirts. I passed the 11-plus and then my mother had to decide between two very different schools. I could have gone to a traditional grammar school in central Dundee with clear-cut rules, an expensive uniform and largely middle-class children. Or I could go to a new comprehensive on the other side of town for which the educational authority was trying hard to recruit brighter children.

My mother didn't see the decision in a wider way. She saw only the new buildings, heard the talk about it being a genuine chance for everyone, more egalitarian. But the new comprehensive was a mistake. I wouldn't have felt threatened by being academic in the grammar school. And I wouldn't have been cut off from the people I had gone to primary school with, neither those who went to the secondary modern, nor the few who had passed the 11-plus as well.

So I was bussed out of the area where I lived, only to confront prejudice against 'brighter' children who read books. In spite of being a very modern comprehensive, the children were strictly streamed. I was in 1A1 which says it all: first year, A stream, top class. There were five classes in the A stream and 13 classes in the B stream. To be ascribed to a certain level at that stage, it was tough going. Looking back it seems just awful that it could happen like that. When I left I was in 3A5, the 5 standing for the Humanities group. Because we were further divided into the Latin/Greek group, the Maths group, the Humanities group, etc. And they thought they were giving everyone an equal chance!

Eventually I started truanting, a lot of sore throats, which were genuine, but they might not have happened if I had been happy. It was a very rough area we were put into, lots of juvenile crime. The children who survived best were those with parents who had made a genuine choice and who were academically supportive.

Both my mother and my brother, eighteen years older, were offered scholarships but couldn't go because their families couldn't afford to keep them there. My mother loved books but she worked long hours which left her so drained she didn't have the energy to explore other things. She worked at a chocolate factory and a battery-making factory. My Gran looked after the house and was a home worker, sewing labels on clothes and getting very little pay for it.

So I was happy and protected at home; home was a safe place to be. But my sights for myself went down year after year as regards the kind of job I'd get. In primary school I thought of going to university or doing a teacher training course. Then in secondary school I thought I'd be a nurse. But by the time I left, as soon as I officially could, I saw only shop work as my destiny. I went to work for an optician in central Dundee. Basically I was a receptionist/fitter of spectacles, working with two older women, again. I go for safety really.

Gran and mother were not surprised when I left school. My mother always said as long as I was happy, it didn't matter what I did. They were quite pleased with a job where I wouldn't get dirty, as I would have if I'd worked in a factory or cleaning.

Would you say schools have changed appreciably since then?

I'd like to think so but the OU has made me very aware of children's early conditioning. For example, my daughter came home from student teaching and told me that Father Christmas had come with magnets for the boys and beads for the girls. In a primary school which prides itself on equal opportunities like making sure girls get as much computer time as boys! My daughter pointed it out to the teacher, but she hadn't noticed it, nobody had. These are the same teachers who think they are very fair and non-sexist.

What does the OU mean to you?

I was doing the 'Changing Experience of Women' course, in which many women become very bitter and resentful of what their lives are like. But my circumstances during the course were that I had to be in hospital to have a hysterectomy. And the OU helped, first in that I went into hospital as a student with TMAs (tutor-marked assignments) to do and books to read. And I wrote about paternalism in medicine; that was my assignment, and it was a life-saver. I observed everything around me and kept my identity through the OU. It was a week of being myself and a person, versus being a patient, dependent and weak. Some of the nurses had been *my* students previously and I gave them advice about their work. I was giving back to these young women.

Summer school personified a lot of what the OU did for me and many others. It allows you to make choices. My identity was severely dented by my hysterectomy and the OU summer school helped me get over not feeling whole. The summer school helped me get over being not only a patient, but an ill person. That goes back to being ill a lot as a child. Being ill was a comfortable escape.

This most recent time in hospital, just months ago, again I needed to have my identity around me, not to give it up and collect it on the way out. This time I was an authority on deafness. I noticed that the rampant paternalism had lessened, the assumptions the gentlemen doctors make about women. It's very odd the way they do not see the whole woman, but see her in a very stereotyped way which disempowers women. I had four days' warning and in those four days I prepared myself in that I got books, tapes, radio, ordered the *Guardian* every day, and in my little bit of the hospital, they stopped cleaning and let me get on with it. The nurses understood where I was coming from, that I wanted to maintain myself. I phoned the office regularly to see if work was being taken care of.

The effect of this really busy bed on the consultant as he made his rounds with students was incredible. He said, 'Of course, *these* women, they won't want to read anything more than the *Women's Weekly*.' And then he looked at my bed and said, 'Well, *this* woman with all the books around her is obviously the exception.' And on that same ward, lots of students were very new to this line of med, the post op, the consultant would say, 'How do you think that woman over there might be feeling?' It made me furious. Why don't you ask her? Why don't you ask me?

I'm on many equal opportunities things in the RNID which is pretty sensitive on gender issues. We have childcare and maternity leave for men as well as women. And I am quite fussy about sexist language. Something was going out from our office that I didn't see, something about manning the office, and I got quite pernickety and it was snatched back and changed before it went out.

How has the OU changed you?

I'm a lot more confident. At summer school I wanted to be there for *me* and I did not want to stick with my tutorial group. I wanted to be in a group where I didn't know anyone, go into it fresh and meet new people. Not that I didn't like the people in my tutorial group but I didn't want the option of them being a safe group.

I've become a person who will lurch into situations that to the outside may be seen as bravery. When my daughter had a psychology assignment having to do with bystander intervention, she said she had only to describe how her mother was likely to behave. I remember the children were embarrassed once when I confronted a teenage boy who was torturing a bird. I felt so angry, I said, 'Don't you dare do that. Let it go.' To anyone on the outside, it would have looked quite brave because he could have turned on me and kicked me and I don't think anyone would have helped.

I was with my boss in a London tube train station travelling from Bath to Peterborough and he said, 'I'll bet you can't get through this journey without getting involved in some emergency.' I said, 'Oh, yes I can.' 'No, you always get into an adventure,' he said, 'I'm just waiting to see what will happen.' And we are standing on this platform, hundreds of people around, and this foursome way far off made this beeline right to us. They actually asked him the questions they had. And he said, 'It's because you're here. It wouldn't have happened if I'd been on my own.' So I must look like someone now who takes risks.

What impact has the OU had on your career?

When the children were young I was involved as a volunteer working in groups with people. I started the OU in 1980 and three years later I got my first job offer. Since then, the OU made me want to stretch the jobs I've had, starting with teaching GCE O-level psychology part-time at the island's College of Arts and Technology. I enjoyed producing appropriate schemes of work and identifying students with individual tutoring needs and then being their coach.

From 1988 to 1992 I've had a three-year contract. I joined as Project Officer and was promoted to Project Manager, managing both the IoW RNID office and the Sound Advice Project. RNID is the biggest charity working in the field of deafness in Britain. I was paid by them for 18 hours work a week doing action research. My initial job was to look at the IoW facilities for the deaf – there had been a very low level of service – and to work with the local social services to learn what deaf people's needs were, and then suggest ways of being proactive in meeting those needs. A year ago I saw an advert that there was money available for people working with volunteers, and I had a week to do the application, based on work I'd done, giving deaf people access to information and equipment. So we applied and we got the money – £60,000 – and were able to set up an RNID office on the island a year ago, the Sound Advice Project based in Newport. So now we have a part-time Environmental Equipment Officer, Volunteer Co-ordinator, Secretary/Administrator, and fifteen volunteers.

My job's almost done. Once the people are able to do the job and other funding comes in, it would be better if I stepped back and left. But this project will be an RNID model for other regions for the way services can be developed in other parts of the country.

Some OU graduates say the OU taught them to see their work differently. Did this happen to you?

The course that changed me the most was a rogue course, TAD292, Technology, Arts & Social Sciences. The ethos behind the TAD course was you built your own hoops and then decided whether you wanted to jump through them or not. For one TMA you couldn't use any words. That course was frightening and most satisfying at the same time.

One of the premises behind it was you should question everything. It encouraged you to go out and find out things for yourself. I questioned people's roles the most. I concluded they were not as fixed as I'd thought. If I go to anything involving OU people now, I can be certain someone will say, 'I'll bet you did that funny course.' Maybe it just attracted people who were like that anyway, open to change and experiences. That's what the OU's done for me, it's made me think I have power.

I'll give you a recent example. In September I joined a writing class for sheer relaxation because the work I am doing is great and exciting, but I tend to sit down in the evening and work. Ten weeks of going to creative writing class, it seemed like good fun. I just wanted to test out more creativity in writing. But the other people are interested in writing for money, writing romantic fiction. The power I got through the OU, specifically through TAD, was that I felt all right going there and saying, 'Okay, I respect what you're doing but it's not what I want to do. I don't want to write romantic novels, but I'm quite interested in putting my own thoughts on paper.' But the bravest thing I did was, we were given the task of writing a synopsis of a Mills & Boon novel. So I looked at a few books that people had brought along, and I looked at the ingredients, and I worked with that, so that when we came to reading our scripts out, mine was quite different from the others. It was only one sheet of A4, and I'd been very naughty . . . it could have been seen as quite insulting given the work that the other people had done, but luckily it went down extremely well. I had looked at the sorts of phrases used in Mills & Boon and had made separate lists from which people could choose. I'd have a sentence like: 'Justine had never felt like this before. She looked up at Charles and . . . ', and then people had a multiple choice of how to finish the action. It was taking the class on my own terms and I got terrific fun out of preparing for that evening. But without the OU and TAD, I would have thought, 'This class isn't for me.'

What is the most important use you make of your OU degree?

Flexibility of thought, consciousness of thinking something through, finding an answer, and recognizing it was the same process we achieved at the OU.

I use all of the content, starting with the Arts and Social Science foundation courses and continuing with personality, education, social psychology. But the confidence it gave me! Back to that TAD course. We had one assignment where we had to go to the National Gallery and ask people why they were there. It was quite a good pick-up station. You can get some very strange answers to, 'Excuse me, would you mind telling me why you are here?' Even if you start with, 'I'm doing an Open University assignment and I just want to ask you a few questions.'

I got so comfortable there I nearly got arrested before my exams. I went back to the Gallery to pass the time and they were searching people's bags randomly because a painting had been slashed and I told them I had nothing, forgetting the craft knife I was carrying, so when they looked in my bag and found it they took me off to a room and interrogated me and I told them I needed it for my OU exam. I thought, What am I leading the OU into? I showed them the papers for the exam, where it was to be held, etc. Afterwards I spoke to another student on a park bench and he told me I was followed by a security guard all the way to the exam hall at the University of London.

Why was the OU right for you?

One way it was right was moving around the country like I did with my husband, it was tailor-made for me. The other way it was right was that I wanted to be home-based in my studies while the children were growing up and because of the different demands of David's job. When I applied to the OU, I thought, If David goes some place where he has afternoons free again, or goes on sabbatical, I want to be able to fit in. That's how it felt, that's how it still feels, flexible in the way it could fit in with a family.

How did you balance your OU studies with your family responsibilities?

I'd get up at 6 and do an hour or two before anyone got up. Another strategy was to work when I had the house all to myself. I tried to study in a way that didn't involve the rest of the family. I tried to keep the weekends clear. At the time I started the OU, I wasn't the only one in the family studying. David was doing a part-time external MPhil with Leeds University. He's now doing a diploma in criminology with the OU and part of his reason for choosing the OU is he's seen how it's worked for me.

What advice would you have for women considering an OU degree?

For someone like me, having set aside my career to bring up my daughters, I would say start gradually. When my first child was a baby I began getting back into education with a taster course, a day to give women a taste of education. I took millinery, English and French. I also began kicking over the traces by learning how to swim and how to drive. Then in 1978 when we were living in Wakefield, I started evening classes. I started with two English O-levels, got an A and a B. And then took maths, sociology and psychology. I also got involved with Asian women, helping them to learn English, and I began to think, Yes, to the idea of the OU.

What was your image of the OU before your studies and after?

When the OU was founded, I started thinking about it. But first I had to do the O-levels, a bit of caution. Because my image was there were these thousands of people all over the country getting up at 4 o'clock in the morning, going off and doing jobs and then coming home and shutting themselves away to study and working very hard. But I also thought it might be second-rate, an easy thing to do. I found the opposite!

What was hardest about studying with the OU and easiest?

Either I've been very lucky or the tutors and counsellors are very good. The times when I've been ill, they've been very supportive and that has always given me the impetus to put more into the OU.

I was one of those people who got very involved. I went to all of the tutorials, weekly or fortnightly. We lived in Acton and David worked at Wormwood Scrubs where he was an assistant governor, a wing governor, and he felt very drained. But he babysat for me, Jane was 9, Kate 6, so one evening each week I could go off to my tutorials. By far the most difficult year was when I was ill and had my hysterectomy, 1985–86. I had the operation in July, but I went to summer school in Norwich five weeks later for the 'Changing Experience of Women' against medical advice. I actually took a letter from my doctor to summer school. But I was so glad I went.

What qualities were responsible for your success?

I am a hard worker, quite conscientious and analytical. I have enthusiasm for studying. I am very open to new ideas and people. I'm also very into detail.

What was most important in your life before the OU and after?

Family. It's still family, but less so. There have been quite a few times in the last years when I put the work I was doing before the immediate needs of the family. And I think my family's wider needs now are better met by me being a more fulfilled person. The OU's been quite a stabilizing thing for me, since I've carried it around the country, but the family also has been stabilizing because I've also carried it around the country as well!

Dale wrote several months after her interview. Her husband had started a new job in the Prison Service HQ in London, one daughter was off to do a degree in Bath, while the other daughter was finishing school and deciding on a university course. 'My life has changed a fair bit since we met earlier this year. I took your advice and had a CV produced. Shortly after your visit I saw a job advertised – fundraising manager of the hospice here. More money than my RNID job and the chance to work for a movement I believe in. So I applied, was successful and changed jobs three months ago.'

I looked over Dale's very impressive CV. No wonder she got her new job! Under 'major responsibilities' for the RNID she listed planning, teamwork, management, fund-raising, literature, campaigns, consultation, publicity, research. And then comes her list of 'achievements'. She's come a long way from a sickly, miserable teenager who shuffled out of a Dundee comprehensive, settling for shop work as her destiny.

Chapter 3

Classed Schools

By increasing class segregation [through parental choice] schools could lose their more able pupils, who might help to create a strong disciplinary climate as well as high academic standards. . . . 'The losers are the lower social class children and also the teachers in those schools. The really sad result is that pupils in predominantly working-class areas don't have any clout and could be marginalized into ghetto schools which have lost their most talented pupils and their resources,' said Professor Willms. (Young, 1992)

'Tell me, Bev,' asked my American accountant innocently over a summer salad, 'how does social class affect a child's education in England?' Oh, oh, I thought as I passed the bread rolls to Bev, a retired primary headmistress, I wonder how she's going to react.

'Well,' the ex-headmistress humphed, 'it doesn't matter what *we* do in the schools. We treat all of the children equally, but social class rules.' Then she went on to tell a story about how she had asked a class of inner-city seven-year-olds who wanted to be Queen, King, the knights, etc., in the Christmas pageant? A pale-faced, poorly dressed little girl raised her hand for Queen and was greeted by hoots and hollers from her classmates. The only girl who could act the part, the children agreed, was Daphne, because only Daphne had the hair, the clothes, the accent, and the standoffishness to be a queen. 'So, at the age of 7,' Bev said, buttering her roll, 'based on social class, peers dictate children's expectations and teachers can't do anything about it.'

Leaving aside the huge socio-economic divide between independent, fee-paying schools and state schools, I get the impression that individual schools everywhere in the UK are stamped as 'middle-class' or 'working-class' depending on what class the majority of students comes from. When the league tables of GCSE examination results were published in 1992, they were accompanied by a flurry of articles saying such things as 'King Edward's pupils come from fairly affluent homes and parents here are very supportive of their children' versus 'St Edmund's children come from an area of 24 per cent unemployment, many single-parent families, inadequate housing, much poverty and ill-health'. This sounds like the 'social-classing' of schools to me.

How do classed schools affect children?

Do teachers in largely working-class primary schools simply give up on their charges from the start? Does the fact that teachers in middle-class primaries expect the bulk of their pupils to be successful in exams determine their future?

No one can doubt the gravity of what goes on in primary schools after reading Liz Heron's (1985) *Truth, Dare or Promise*, twelve stories about girls and school. Ten of Heron's twelve women were able to lift themselves out of the working class by attending middle-class schools. The Academy, the Convent, the Parli, and Epsom County Grammar School for Girls meant they wouldn't be waitresses; these schools meant they'd get good jobs or go to university.

One of the twelve, Julia Pascal, recalled when the examination results came out. 'About half the class has passed and I am one. The other half pretend I-don't-care-never-wanted-to-go-to-grammar-school-anyway. I feel happy that I am one of the chosen. I'm going to be a Collegiate girl and go to the red-brick school on the hill. Many of the others are crying. It's as if someone has ripped the class in half, and those small children thrown out from the chance of grammar school education know deep in their hearts that this is the crucial moment in their lives. . . . It's not anything they can articulate, just a knowledge that their new place in a secondary modern makes sure that for the rest of their lives they will feel secondary.'

In Liz Heron's days, a primary school's social class determined how much attention the school focused on the children to do well in the 11-plus exam. Today, with national curriculum tests as early as 7, are people's futures sealed when they have barely started school?

The newspapers have told me that there are only 159 grammar schools left in the UK, *but* opting out has emboldened another 200 schools to try for it. Will they be like Devon's Colyton Grammar School, described as 'mainly white middle-class'? Colyton Grammar now actually pays primary schools to administer the 11-plus and gets them to compete with one another to see which can produce the most 'winners' (Strickland, 1992).

How does a school's social class affect teenagers and young adults?

Here are just three examples of possible class-linked learning environments. First, a girls' boarding school:

> For seven years you were with exactly the same type of girl from exactly the same type of background as you. We were the children of fourth or fifth generation public school parents, who placed great importance on status. An important but unspoken part of things was that your father was something in the City, and you had a house in the country and a flat in Chelsea. (Berridge, 1992)

Then there is the north London comprehensive described in my local paper. It has 900 children of both sexes. All levels of intelligence are taught in mixed-ability groups which include children with special educational needs. There are no special sets for any subjects. It has very high standards of achievement, but also a high turnover of students, many of whom haven't been in the country very long. For over half, English is not their first language. It is difficult to put a label on this school, but no one would say it's middle-class.

Last, there are the students at two outright working-class comprehensives in Middleport, South Wales, described by Phillip Brown in the 1980s. The students are of three types – 'rems', 'swots' and 'ordinary kids'. The rems reject school, the swots accept it and the ordinary kids just want to become respectable working-class adults. In the period before O-level and CSE examinations had been superseded by the GCSE, that meant passing CSEs. Then boys would enter craft apprenticeships and girls low-level clerical and service jobs. O-levels had nothing whatever to do with their future lives, commented Brown.

Does this classed school obstacle affect our education as adults?

Yes, because the more working-class the school that you go to, the less likely you are to get more education as an adult. Jane French (1990) says that the strides made by girls over the past twenty years in catching up with their brothers have been made by middle-class girls. For working-class girls, from the lower bands and streams of secondary school, very little has changed. Thus, as adults, it's middle-class women who go on to further education and working-class women who stay employed in shops, factories and offices.

How serious is this obstacle today?

I think it is a serious problem when an educator like Jane French (1990), in a book of advice for the parents of daughters, tells them to take a good look at catchment areas when selecting schools. Two schools can be near one another and yet have very different records of achievement, and 'this happens because of the relationship of social class to education attainment. Put very simply, the children of unskilled manual workers have far less chance of doing well at school and going on to university than the children of highly qualified professional people' (p. 59).

Elsewhere I read that in 1988 men in Social Class I were 11 times more likely to get a degree than men in Social Class V, while women in Social Class I were *13 times* more likely to get a degree than women in Social Class V. In 1989 the chances of someone from Social Class I entering university were 18 times greater than for someone from Social Class V. So this class connection to higher education is indisputable (Corrigan, 1992).

Indisputable, too, is the *classed-school* connection to higher education. As Professor Willms says, working-class children are hurt when middle-class students and their educational values migrate elsewhere. It means the working-class children's chances of going on to higher education have been weakened.

But the migrating middle-class students are hurt as well, aren't they? Now they will learn far less about the real world of many cultures, clashing values and different ideas about what's important in life.

> Of course, life feels much easier for individuals if they don't have to negotiate cultural and ethnic diversity, especially at the moment, when poverty and urban deprivation affect different groups to such different degrees. Such divisions are uncomfortable. Children in mixed schools do not necessarily mix, and when they do they often ask uncomfortable questions, or pick up habits not wanted in 'nice' middle-class homes. (Coward, 1993)

The story in the following chapter illustrates how women's aspirations for higher education are affected by the class of their schools. Viv Steers' family was working-class, but she attended a state grammar school that, to some degree, rewarded academic success. The problem for Viv was that this school emphasized O-levels and producing people to work for banks and offices. So like her classmates, Viv got a job. Later she did her A-levels at a technical college, became a pharmacist and entered the middle class. It wasn't until the OU that Viv began to think through what social class was all about.

Chapter 4

Viv Steers

From Pharmacist to English Language Teacher

I really did think when I was a pharmacist and my ex-husband was a banker, that if you weren't in banking or you weren't in pharmacy, you weren't worth even considering. And when I told my mother that I was going to marry John, she said, 'Oh, I wish you could have married a solicitor or a doctor.' She thought in marrying a carpenter, I hadn't done the right thing for myself. And she was an ordinary working-class lady! Perhaps we haven't all had the same advantage, money-wise or family-wise, but that doesn't make us inferior people. That is what I did learn. Everybody has their own place, an important place, in life. So it's quite a big thing to say, but I certainly wouldn't have married John without having done the Open University.

This was Viv's final statement, just before our husbands, several friends and a pack of dogs tumbled into their Mallorcan living room to end our interview and start a rollicking ride towards a Christmas Eve lunch.

I travelled the farthest on this project to interview Viv in response to this letter (and I'll admit, the promise of sunshine):

> I qualified as a pharmacist in 1960 at age 23 and married shortly after. My marriage broke up in 1974 (no children). In 1978 I took a lease on a pharmacy and also commenced OU studies (D101). I started with 2 credits due to my previous qualification. In 1985 I was awarded the OU BA degree after studying courses in the Social Sciences including The Changing Experience of Women in Society. I had re-married in 1981.
>
> In 1987 both of my parents and my mother-in-law died. We had a holiday flat here and my husband, a carpenter, was finding the do-it-yourself syndrome in the UK affecting his business so we moved here to live in 1988. Foreigners cannot work here as employed, only self-employed. This was fine for my husband but for me things were not so jolly. Retirement was not my cup of tea.
>
> In March I am going on a course to learn to teach English as a Foreign Language. The diploma I shall obtain together with my degree will be sufficient to obtain a work permit as a teacher of English. I never thought that the OU studies and qualification would be of help job-wise. I did it for the challenge and to meet new friends. But here I am 53 and embarking on a new career.

An OU graduation photo was among many mementoes on display in Viv's high-ceilinged living room in their house on a steep hillside above Son Servera. It showed a diminutive, plump, smiling, white-haired woman in cap and gown. Viv and I sat on velvet sofas facing one another, while an old dog snored in a basket by the wood fire. The house was neatly arranged, reflecting Viv's style, while John's shop was cluttered and laid-back, John's style.

You said your reason for studying with the OU was for the challenge and to meet new friends. Do you want to elaborate?

I got started with the Open University in 1978, the same year I bought my own pharmacy near Croydon. The husband of an employee complained how much OU studies took up of her husband's time and I thought, I could do with something that took up my time.

First I did a half-credit associate course on the rise of science and technology in the last century, something I thought I knew something about. Everything connected with it was enjoyable. When I was later accepted by the OU, I started with the social science foundation course, taking advantage of pre-course lectures at the Croydon Centre. Probably the most memorable part of D101 was summer school at Nottingham University, where I thought, This is what I should have done when I was 18. Gone to university. Lived on campus. Joined the Debating Society. Then I would have known who I was, what I wanted to know, and didn't want to know. I would have got it all out of my system.

So my original motivation for the OU was the same as my motivation after we moved to the island: I had time on my hands and was mentally bored. I wanted something to do in the evenings besides watch television. I don't enjoy things other people enjoy, sport, sewing, knitting. But I found I did enjoy studying. And when I realized I could get a degree, it gave me a goal to work for. I'd like to go on distance learning for its own sake forever, even if I have a job where I'm using my degree in a practical sense. I'd like to get a distance-learning doctorate, if it were possible, just to prove that people from humble circumstances can do it if they have the determination.

What obstacles or constraints did you have to succeeding with the OU?

I was an only child and my parents both came from big working-class families in which both lost their fathers. Consequently, my parents' education was very basic, but they *had* to read and write properly. Although my mother was a brilliant pianist, she became a dressmaker. My father was a butcher all his life. They were good people. They didn't do a good deal in their lives but they cared very much about me, their home, and their garden. They saved up their money and took holidays abroad. They loved going abroad, sitting outside a bar, having a coffee in the sunshine; they thought that was wonderful. That's how I got my love of going abroad. But my parents didn't push me to do well, their attitude being, 'You'll do what you can do.'

I did pass a scholarship at 11 and attended a state grammar school. I enjoyed the competition of the school and got a kind of high from doing well in examinations that has stayed with me all my life. I left school at 16, taking O-levels in the two Englishes, French, mathematics, history, geography, biology and domestic science. My school didn't turn out people to go to university, it turned out people to work in banks and insurance offices. And when I said I wanted to be a pharmacist – because it looked interesting – I was told, 'Oh, no, you can't do that because you have to have chemistry and physics, and of course, only boys do chemistry and physics. Girls do biology.' In my life that has become a very important thing to me: that in those days, girls had no choice. I'm not a great feminist but there were a lot of very bad things done in girls' education in England then. If you didn't pass that scholarship at 11, you didn't go to a grammar school that could prepare you for university. You went to an ordinary secondary modern school, and all you could do from there was typing, hairdressing, or work in a shop. You had no qualifications whatsoever. So at 11 years old, your future was decided for you by the education system.

Then when I wanted to do A-levels so I could go into pharmacy, my father wasn't very keen. His attitude was that I would get married and have children and the education would be wasted. My mother finally persuaded him to fill out the grant forms even though he didn't want to declare his income. He didn't even want his wife to know how much he earned, let alone the authorities. So that was my first battle coming up against men who didn't approve of women studying and having careers.

What does the OU mean to you? How has it changed your life?

One of the most influential OU courses was Crime and Society, which led to my becoming a magistrate. After listening to lectures on the prison system, I thought, It shouldn't be left to people with time on their hands. Ordinary people like me should be involved in all this, people who didn't go to public schools. So eventually I did become a magistrate, after I got married to John in 1981. I told the people in the PTA at school that I was interested, so they put me forward and I was a magistrate for three years before we came here to live in 1988. That's the only thing I miss. I would have missed the Open University, too, but I found out luckily I could do that here.

I had sold my business, the children were at school and I was taking a half-credit OU course. I was also working on a part-time basis in private pharmacies three or four days a week. When I was appointed a magistrate, I could work whatever three days I liked. Magistrates are meant to be a cross-section of society, but in a lot of jobs, lots of people couldn't be a magistrate, particularly in lower-paid unskilled jobs. They'd either be ostracized by their workmates or their bosses would make life difficult. It's balanced with men and women, politically, and it's balanced socially. But it's only certain classes of people that can afford to give this time free. So if you live in a very, very working-class area, you will find the people on the bench are from the big houses and the higher classes and the people who can manage to have the time off. If you're a factory foreman or a railway porter, it's not convenient to the employer for you to have a day off work, so in my mind the biggest problem is the under-representation of unskilled or skilled workers. Yet some of the best magistrates came from unions, where they learned how to think and see both sides of a question.

But perhaps the biggest change my social sciences courses prepared me for was to leave the closed world of pharmacy and, ultimately, England. For one, I am not in favour of pharmacists and industrialists making so much money out of medicines, when illnesses can be treated with much simpler things that cost far less. I felt I was dishing out drugs and medicines that were just draining the country. And that thinking came from studying with the Open University, studying social subjects and learning about different ways of looking at things. People have been urging me, now that it is 1992, to go back to pharmacy here in Mallorca, but I don't want to. I believe pharmacy and medicine have taken a very bad turn in the Western world.

Furthermore, the professional aspect has disappeared from chemists' shops and they are now indistinguishable from sweet-shops and veg shops and everything else shops. When I was trained, it was to treat illness; pharmacists know how to treat illnesses. And when I was a hospital pharmacist I used to go on rounds with the doctors, prescribing for what the doctors were diagnosing. Doctors diagnose, pharmacists treat. That is what this qualification was all about.

Can you give me an example from Mallorcan life of this ability to see both sides of things that the OU teaches?

Not many English people understand what culture means, that is, they are unaware that there is any other way of living but their way. And just as the Raj in India imposed British culture, the British in Mallorca try to impose their ideas upon others and dismiss Mallorcan attitudes as wrong. For example, there is a difference in the definition of truth. Westerners think a thing is either true or untrue. But because of the Moorish influence upon Mallorca, they don't see truth the same as the Western world. They will tell you what they think you want to hear. So if you say, 'My television needs repairing. How long will it take?' they'll say, 'Two days.' They'll say what you want them to say. But it never is repaired in two days, and it has nothing to do with mañana. So you go back in two days, and they'll say, 'Oh, it's not ready. Tomorrow.' And you could be doing that for six weeks. And the British get aggravated and angry. We used to. The police said our permits could be collected in three weeks, so in duly English fashion, in three weeks we were there. But we wouldn't do it now. We'd wait six weeks and say, 'Well, we'd better go to Palma now and see if they're ready.'

And if you're in a shop waiting to be served and a lady comes in and starts chatting to the assistant, you just stand there. And get angry. But they're not doing that because you're a foreigner, that's the way they do it. They have not been subjected to the rat race. Ten minutes waiting is not that important. It is important to earn money to live on, but to have all the material things that we in Britain consider important? No, they don't think like that. Home is important and every day is important. If I said to my friends, 'In a fortnight's time, will you come to dinner?' they'd say, 'Will you ask us again three days before, because we can't think that far ahead.'

Some OU graduates say it taught them to see things differently. Was this true for you?

When we got married and I moved into John's house, because everyone came inside by the side door, we put a big desk in an unused front hallway for my study area. However, one day a colleague of John's did knock and I answered with 'Oh, excuse me, I'm just studying lesbianism and you'll find John in the kitchen making jam.' He never looked at us the same after that. But I was far more shaken that he was by what I was studying: The Changing Experience of Women.

I wasn't radical enough for that summer school. I had never encountered before in my life a lesbian who lived in the red-light district of Bristol who was the mother of a 2-year-old whom she breastfed in the refectory. I had never heard stories from women who wouldn't give the names of their children to social services, and were locked in rooms and badgered about the men in their lives. It made me think, My God, this is the world I live in! This is the real world. But I was pleased to have heard it because these things happen. But more disturbing than certain individuals' lifestyles was the deep antagonism these women felt towards men. They truly wanted a revolution. They wanted to overturn society and bring it in line with what they believed and their antipathy towards men went so far as to deny the men on the course all-men groups. My point of view, that it is nice to have men around as friends at the very least, was not tolerated. And the strength of the women's beliefs about discrimination was as strong as other people's religious beliefs. But as that week passed, I came to understand their views better and now among our acquaintances I get labelled 'the red under the bed' because I try to see both sides of every question.

What's the most important use you make of your OU degree?

Well, the most recent, practical use is that I wrote the newsletter for the ESRA, English Speaking Residents' Association, for the north-east district of the island. The OU made me a better writer and I did the newsletter as long as I could do it for pleasure. I only quit when it became a power struggle over what should go in and what shouldn't go in. The ESRA has a proper constitution and is registered with the Spanish authorities as a charitable organization. It is a very British thing. How and why did Britain become imperialistic? Because they are like this. They have this, 'We all do it together and we're British and we've got to keep everything together, chaps, otherwise it might not be a good thing.' For example, look at this item from last April: 'Navy Ships: Many of you will know that when British Navy ships are in port, requests are made for residents to offer some form of hospitality to members of their crew. In the past, most offers have come from people living in the Palma area. However, our British Consul would like hospitality to be offered by ex-pats living in other parts of the island. This hospitality would then be reciprocated in some way on the ship concerned. The ship currently in dock is the *Ark Royal*. More information is available.'

Why was the OU right for you?

Because I needed a goal and each course meant I was getting nearer to that goal, a degree. Some people do a university course to better themselves, but I did it to make myself a better person, able to see both sides of social and political problems. One of the things they said to me was, when I went for my interview to be a magistrate, 'Do you think that if there were three magistrates, and two felt differently from you, you would be able to change your mind?' 'Yes,' I said, 'if they explained why they felt as they did, I could.' And they said, 'That's good. We need people who can change their minds easily.' But I was raised to see changing my mind easily as weak.

One of the cases we had, we had to say whether there was a case to answer, a man accused of sexually assaulting his stepdaughter. And when the barrister stands up and gives the details, they are quite nasty and horrific. But at the end, when you've heard all the sides, and he wasn't an eloquent man, just the opposite, a simple man who portrayed his feelings in the way he knew, we said there was a case to answer, but we didn't think he was guilty. And in the end, the jury did find him not guilty.

What's the most important ingredient to women's success at the OU?

Faith in yourself. To get it you've got to speak to other people who have done it. People who can tell you that it isn't watching television. People who can tell you what units and TMAs and summer schools are, and how much study is involved. Go along to a tutorial. Take a returning-to-school course. See that people in their seventies and eighties, people without even a basic education, can do it and will tell you it is worth doing. Because I found out at my graduation that the OU degree is the third or fourth most respected degree in Britain. But to embark on it, you've got to have faith in yourself, especially if you are somebody who has everything against you, such as a husband who says, 'Not in my house'. Because the OU's not something to dabble in.

Why would you advise other women to do an OU degree?

Because it opens doors. After I left school I was an apprentice for Boots the Chemist, working and studying in their own dispensing course. Then the next two years I spent at Croydon Technical College taking chemistry, physics and biology A-levels, working holidays and Saturdays at Boots for extra money. Then I proceeded to Chelsea School of Pharmacy where two courses were offered, the two-year Pharmaceutical Chemist course and the three-year Bachelor of Pharmacy course. The bachelor's course was for people who wanted to work in industry or do research. At that point I only wanted to work in a chemist's shop, I didn't think I was good enough to do research, and so I took the Pharmaceutical Chemist course. Not a degree. This is important. Because in life, once one has a degree, it opens doors. And it doesn't matter what degree. And it doesn't matter when you get it.

What were the hardest and easiest aspects to studying with the OU?

When doing summer schools, I would think, This is all too easy, a bit of a waste. I wonder what the reason for doing this is? But when I got home, months later, even years later, I would realize what I had got out of something I had seen as easy. I remember a course on Making Sense of Society. Each summer school group had a coach trip round Nottingham to study how towns were constructed. In the town centre was industry, and around it was a ring that was the shopping and commercial area, and then a ring round that where the lower classes lived, and with the ever-expanding concentric rings the social structure changed. So we were to study Nottingham with this ring model in mind. But my group just happened to do it on the day of the royal wedding between Prince Charles and Diana. There wasn't a soul anywhere. It was like a ghost town with everybody in the city watching the television.

We felt as though they shouldn't be there. We couldn't observe the areas as we were intended to. The bustling industrial bit, for instance, was completely shut up. And as we drove through the working-class part of the town, it was like eavesdropping to see the trestles with tablecloths being spread out and garlands strung in preparation for street parties. But what we saw by chance, instead of how towns are constructed, was how towns continue to be cemented together through religious and social ritual. The royal family was gluing communities together as they had for centuries. Everybody had been given the day off to celebrate this wedding and as our coach wound through the deserted streets of rich and poor areas alike, celebrating was exactly what everybody was doing.

Why were you successful with the OU?

I tie it to early school successes. My mother would give me a new notebook if I came second in history or third in the class. I wasn't good at much else, not much good at art or sport or doing things with my hands. I enjoyed learning new things back then, and I rediscovered that delight with the OU. I got the same satisfaction out of learning what capitalism meant as other people get out of a good round of golf or knitting a beautiful jumper.

What are your plans?

In addition to teaching English, I have now embarked on my honours degree by taking two half-credit courses, DE325 Work and Society, and DE354 Beliefs and Ideology, and I'm looking forward to two more half-credit courses, one concerning revolutions and one Europe and the Common Market. I'll take my exams in Palma at the British Institute.

What was most important in your life before and after the OU?

Before it was the home, being a wife, and earning money to go away on holidays and for my husband to have the clothes and things he wanted. It was very shallow and would have been boring except that my work brought me into contact with the public. What is most important *now* is that the OU gave me something I can do for the rest of my life, learning can be my friend, all my life. Like I have said, I have found something I get a kick out of. Middle age does not mean coming towards the end; it can be a beginning.

I want to enjoy life, to live in the present and in the future, and it is this side of my nature where the OU comes in. The OU has nothing to do with the past. It is a forward thing, happening now, always enjoyable and entertaining.

During the last fifteen minutes of the interview the front door must have opened fifteen times. Dogs nosed their way in, friends knocked, husbands tiptoed into the kitchen and back out again. It was getting time to turn the tape recorder off.

Our party drove to a restaurant I never would have noticed, and if I had, I would never have driven in. It looked like a greasy take-out. But inside there were clean-scrubbed wooden tables and cane chairs. Men in workclothes were wolfing down huge bowls of steaming paella. Enormous platters of macaroni, skate and vegetables, pork cutlets and french fries were being passed around. We didn't order. We just sat there and smiled, and the owners beamed and served course after course while Christmas music emanated from the telly.

Viv's last letter said: 'I am thinking of doing a Natural Health course by correspondence, this includes aromatherapy, herbal medicine, reflexology, etc. It would fit in with my pharmaceutical qualification. I see these techniques as "supplementary" to normal medicine. Stress and anxiety have been very neglected areas of medical treatment except via anti-depressant drugs, which are addictive and zombie-making. If I get the diplomas we will buy a small apartment in town where I can practise. My OU experience will have added the necessary psychology and understanding aspect of such health care.'

So perhaps Viv will return to pharmacy after all. But not to the bustling London counters of Boots the Chemist.

Chapter 5

Streaming

At Harborough Primary School the 11-plus exam was not marked in the usual way by the headmistress herself, after the children had gone home. The papers were exchanged with Saxford Tye Primary. This gave the necessary guarantee of impartiality to the closely observant little town, or, as Mrs Traill put it, saved her from being torn to pieces after it was over. She was, perhaps, not quite so sensitive in the matter of giving out the results. The acceptances from Flintmarket Grammar School came in square white envelope. Those from the Technical came in long buff-coloured ones. Each child in the top form, when they arrived at school that summer's morning, looked at their own desk, saw their envelope, and knew their destiny at once. So, too, did everyone else in the class.

Harborough children, looking back in future years over a long life, would remember nothing more painful or more decisive than the envelopes waiting on the desks. (Penelope Fitzgerald, 1978, p.101)

As I understand it, the Education Act of 1976 was supposed to get rid of Harborough's kind of streaming, that is, sending children to grammar schools or secondary moderns based on examination results. So why did I read that in 1992 there were still 159 grammar schools in existence, and that the first grammar school to open in 20 years might well do so, in, of all places, Milton Keynes? And why is the 'Thorne Scheme' alive and well in North Yorkshire (Baird, 1992)? Under the Thorne scheme the 'top' pupils go to grammar school, a decision based not just on examinations, but on essays, teachers' opinions, and, for the borderline cases, long interviews!

Be that as it may, judging from my reading, widespread streaming goes on everywhere *within schools*. It seems commonplace to divide pupils up into different groups based on presumed differences in ability. What is the experience of within-school streaming like for young women?

> We were expected to compete with each other and to this end we were streamed, even before we actually set foot in the school, into A, B and C streams. We were not tested or evaluated by the school, the streaming was based entirely on our 11-plus results. Moreover, there was no liberal nonsense about A, B or C 'just' being letters of the alphabet: the A stream knew it was the A stream as surely as the C stream knew its own place in the world. . . . This streaming

was further reinforced by the allocation to the A stream of teachers who were known to be heads of department or senior staff or teachers of subjects the school regarded as important. The first year C stream thus had as its form teacher a notably incompetent teacher of domestic science, while their contemporaries in the A stream were greeted each morning by the ex-Oxford Head of English. (Mary Evans, 1991, p.11)

How extensive is streaming today?

Two American educators, John Chubb and Terry Moe (1992), commissioned by the *Sunday Times*, said that the 1988 Education Reform Act introduced three important reforms: (1) LMS, or local management of schools, whereby schools could opt out of their local education authorities (LEAs); (2) a national curriculum; and (3) new tests to replace the GCSEs.

Chubb and Moe favour schools opting out on the grounds that such schools can then stream and place poor, inner-city students in technical and vocational courses, and, at the same time, can go right on offering A-level programmes that require tests to get into and good grades to get out of. They defend their philosophy by using the example of a minority pupil at a school in a run-down part of Birmingham who had 'won a place in the top "A-stream" class, a system which was set up four years ago for the most able pupils. Children have to pass tests in English, mathematics and general knowledge to secure a place in the class, where they are set the target of achieving at least eight "pass" grades in their GCSE exam'.

Chubb and Moe began their article by stating: 'The symbols of elitism – the 11-plus exam and the grammar schools – are long gone as foundations of British education.' Really? I wonder what the vocational and technical classmates of this 'more able' student would have to say.

But don't streamed classes receive equal shares of a school's resources?

I have my doubts. An article by a Hampshire teacher, Roger Lowman (1992), describes how streaming works through fictitious Barchester High School for Girls. He recalls a meeting with a couple, a Dr and Mrs Brown, who were pleased that their daughter Amanda had done well on her A-levels:

> But I see their faces cloud over slightly when we speak about Sonia, who took her A-levels here two years ago. Sonia . . . would not have counted as a high-achiever. With her ACC profile, rather than her sister's AAB, she would have been a liability to the school in the percentage table. And their faces cloud over again when I ask about Mary, their younger daughter, who has learning difficulties. We didn't have room for her at Barchester High – such girls devastate our examination percentage rates – so she attends her local comprehensive.

Lowman then goes on to say that Mary will not get 'good' examination grades, meaning she'll get three or four C grades at GCSE, 'and as the school reduces its provision of special needs teaching and spends more on its clever pupils, Mary is less likely to get those three or four'. Mr Lowman blames the league tables for 'coercing' schools, presumably *non*-fictitious ones, into putting money and resources in the top streams at the expense of average and less-than-average students. So we need to know: how widespread is this inequitable division of school resources?

Pauline Swindells, whom I chose for one of the two stories to illustrate the effects of streaming, said quite bluntly that her streaming began in primary school where the children who were thought capable of passing the 11-plus were placed in one class, and the ones thought incapable were sent to another class, and the predictions were a self-fulfilling prophecy, because 'if you went into the right class, then you got all the practice for doing the 11-plus'. Pauline passed it and proceeded to a strict high school that also was streamed. The uniform, the restrictions of what she could and couldn't do, meant that once she had passed her O-levels at 15, she was out of there.

Streaming affects young men the same as young women, doesn't it?

Streaming affects young men, certainly, but not in the same way. Ellen Davies, my other streaming example, failed the 11-plus but got into a girls' grammar school a year later where she was immediately streamed. If she had been placed in the Latin stream, she would have taken physics, chemistry and biology. To her dismay, she was placed in Arts, where she studied general science. I wonder – if she had been a boy in a boys' grammar school, would the same thing have happened?

I know, I know. Ellen is merely a case study of how streaming might affect a woman's highest qualification when she leaves school. But government statistics suggest a similar situation *for all women*. In 1989, among 16- to 24-year-olds, GCE A-levels had been achieved by 30 per cent of males but only 23 per cent of females, while O-levels had been achieved by 37 per cent of females versus 27 per cent of males (Department of Education and Science, 1991, p. xxi).

So I ask, are young men achieving higher levels of qualifications because boys are more likely to be streamed into the O-levels they need for the A-levels they desire?

Chapter 6

Pauline Swindells

From Electronic Engineer to Project Co-ordinator

My OU degree means that doors open. For example, I met this woman in the recruitment department who is assigned to career development and she gave me this list of people to go see. It gives you a very impressive CV if you've got this list of courses that you've done in your own time. You say, 'I have a BA,' and they say, 'You obviously work hard.' The staff department would not have taken so much trouble over things like passing my CV around to various departments if I hadn't done the OU. In the sense that you can tailor it to your own requirements, it is one of the best degrees that you can get in the country.

I interviewed Pauline twice in the evening at a little table in a small room off a tiny kitchen in the flat she owns on the ground floor of a two-storey house. Her pretty, personable cat, Colette, sat on my lap playing with my pen, pens being her favourite thing. Pauline is a single white female, short and thin with straight red hair. She looks years younger than 50, and was in the midst of yet another course, this one in management.

She was born in 1941, grew up in Stockport, her family was working-class, she has three much older siblings. Pauline passed the 11-plus and took a string of O-levels at 15 after which she trained to be a secretary. She then worked for the BBC as a film assistant. She became an electronics technician after two government training courses. She began working for Reuters in 1980 and has risen from field technician to engineer to project co-ordinator. Her OU studies began in 1982 and she got her degree in 1990. She is now working on her honours credits.

What were your reasons for pursuing an OU degree?

After I'd done two government training courses and learned all these things that I didn't know about, but wanted to, and I had my first electronics job, I decided to do O-level physics at night. I won the college prize, which spurred me on. And I did some day releases to get a technology certificate in the 1970s before I worked at Reuters. Then I was going out with somebody who was doing the OU and he gave me the idea, so I took the maths foundation course in 1982. And that was fantastic. I have not taken the OU at a galloping pace, just a steady pace, never more than one unit a year.

After maths foundation and pure maths, I got interested in computers at Reuters, so I did a programming course, databases, a second programming course, and then I did the science foundation course towards the end.

I started it for fun, not for a degree. I met this very nice girl called Tania on the maths foundation course, and we took that and the pure maths together. She lived just around the corner. We did everything together, our tutorials, our TMAs, summer school, and had a very good time. And then we started to do computing, but it wasn't what she wanted, so she dropped out. But I kept going. You get to a certain stage and you think, Well, I've got this far. It's stupid not to get a degree now.

What obstacles to educational success did you have to overcome?

They were very early ones. Streaming was severe in those days, even in primary school. People the teachers thought were going to pass the 11-plus went into one class, and the ones they thought wouldn't pass went into another class, and their predictions were a self-fulfilling prophecy. If you went into the right class, then you got all the practice for doing the 11-plus and I just managed to scrape in because the teacher thought I was a borderline case. I did pass the 11-plus and went to my first choice of school, Fylde's Lodge High School, quite a strict school that also was streamed.

I did O-levels, took them when I was 15, English language and literature, history, French, biology, geography, Latin, maths. My older sister remembers a tremendous battle about whether I should go to university or not, but I don't remember any battle, simply because I didn't want to be at school any more. I didn't want the restriction of a uniform, restrictions of what you could and couldn't do. I had no plans or ideas of what I did want to do, except this idea that I should go to secretarial college. Because I'd done French, I got into Manchester College of Commerce where they gave languages and the aim was to make you into a high-class secretary and translator.

Later, when I was 18, my sister persuaded me I should be going to university, that I'd made a terrible mistake in my life and I should do A-levels, so I started to do A-levels by correspondence, three A-levels in a year. I mean it was impossible. Especially when you're 18, running around all night going to jazz clubs. I tried to do French, Spanish, and English. I got English but I didn't get French and Spanish so I didn't get into university.

Later, during my training courses in electronics, it was a real mind blow. I discovered a lot of things about myself which I didn't know: I liked maths very much; I could do things with my hands; science wasn't so dreadful after all. There was a whole range of things I had ignored at school for various reasons, because basically there was no science teacher at my school, an all-girls school. There was one woman who came in my third year who was a physicist who also had to teach chemistry. She wasn't very good at either and was obviously overstretched because she was the only person in the school who could teach any kind of subject like that. And she wasn't very positive about it as a subject, so it was never very popular.

As far as I know, streaming was to change quite radically with comprehensive education. The whole basis of comprehensive education was more equality of opportunities. No matter what your roots were, you had an equal chance through education of achieving the best that you could. There was a more or less enthusiastic response depending on the local government authority involved. Now we have had a radical swing back since then with the Tory government. And what's happening now with the National Curriculum, they're saying that streaming is a good thing again. Led by the government, we're veering back towards a more elitist way of doing things.

How did the OU change your life?

It's a whole kind of ethos. It means I've got a better job. It does kind of take over your whole life, a lot of your spare time is taken up. If you're not reading, you're phoning someone up, or going to a tutorial, going out for drinks. The year I had off, 1990, from the OU, was the year I moved from engineering to development. I concentrated solely on getting a new kind of a job and I achieved that.

The famous DT200, Technological and Social Implications of Information Technology, opened my eyes to the social aspects of my work and, also, this feeling that as an engineer, you're looked down upon. I'd always got on well with the journalists, but I knew that they saw a person with a screwdriver and that's all they saw. This course motivated me to stretch my wings a bit.

So I applied for a job in development within Reuters. If you take a new job on the outside, you take a huge drop in pay and I had done that once in my life, going from films earning a fair whack, to earning nothing doing a training course. And, of course, now I had a mortgage and a much different lifestyle. Yeah, I thought, why not start at the top, see what happens.

I was quite happy with the interview. So what I did was phone up after the interview – I knew I hadn't got the job – and found out *why* I hadn't got it. I had a nice chat with the woman who was the main interviewer. 'It was a good interview,' she said, 'but it just so happened that there was somebody who had project management experience and he obviously had more relevant experience than you did, so we gave him the job.'

But as a result of that, the staff department knew that I was looking for something and steered me on to another manager, and lo and behold, I got a phone call saying, 'We've seen your CV. Would you like to come over for an interview?' Had a completely and utterly different interview that lasted about twenty minutes. He said, 'This is what we want someone to do,' and gave me a piece of paper, 'Do you think you could do that?' And I said, 'Yeah, I'm sure I could.' It was working on another editorial system. 'Then all you need to do', he said, 'is send me something you've written.' Luckily I had written things, like instructions, documentation, for technicians when I'd been at Fleet Street, so I got the job.

It only lasted 14 months and then they decided to bring the project to an end. This was a horrible shock, absolutely terrible. Because at the time they were also doing a big redundancy scheme and I was thinking, Ohh, this is the end of Reuters. But they said, 'No, it's just the end of a project, like all projects in development. Don't worry, we'll pass your CV around to other managers. What areas would you like to work in?' Within a month I got a response from the man I'm now working for. He wanted a project co-ordinator. I had an even quicker interview with him. Ten minutes and I had the job.

It's a totally different area, on the financial side. Which is why I've been doing this course, an overview of all the financial markets.

Are there any other impacts of your OU studies on your career?

Although I've done computing courses, like the digital computer, and programming courses, none of them were directly relevant. What they did give me was confidence about computing. I would never have gone for the engineer's job if I hadn't have done those programming and computing courses. Without that good basic grounding, I wouldn't have had the confidence.

The last course I did was Managing in Organizations. There are three systems courses, and after my year off, I thought, Am I going to do honours? If so, what? I noticed Working with Systems and so I went to the registration meeting and had a conversation with a woman there who told me about Managing in Organizations, which I had skipped over, thinking that, you know, managing couldn't be relevant to me. And it suddenly clicked, that this was the perfect path. Having then looked at the Managing in Organizations syllabus, I thought, Wow, for the kind of job I'm doing, it would be brilliant. I might be getting a bit old, but I'm not thinking of retiring, and although I won't be going into the upper echelons of management, everybody's got to do some kind of management.

Has your OU degree taught you to see your work differently?

Not only DT200, Introduction to Information Technology, opened my eyes to the social aspects of my work, but also Managing in Organizations. You can't think of a solution to a problem solely in technical terms, you've got to think of it in a holistic way. Who are the people who are going to use the system? How are they going to use it? Why are they going to use it? What are they going to use it for? You don't want a gap between the users and the technologists; the further these two groups are apart, the more difficult it is. Journalists come from an entirely different culture, they have an entirely different idea of how they want to work.

I saw others' attitudes towards me change from when I went around to the journalists' terminals, finding out what their problems were, fixing them, the kind of job where you arrive with a screwdriver. From that I went over to development but I was still working on editorial systems, which are what journalists use to write stories. I was involved in a demonstration of a new system and afterwards four people came to me and said, 'You're transformed. You look entirely different. You behave differently. I can talk to you as an equal now.' Because the demonstration showed I was knowledgeable about the developmental aspects of the system, their whole attitude towards me changed.

What is the most important use you make of your OU degree?

It was extremely instrumental in me moving from engineering to development. Just the mere fact that I had got a degree, and I obviously worked very hard to get it. Incidentally, with a lot of support from Reuters, financial and time off.

But this last course is incredibly relevant for anybody who works for or with anybody else, anywhere else. What it does is teach you about all the kinds of things that happen within an organization, right from the personal up to the multi-national level. It gives you 'tools for thought' about how to work within an organization, so you don't have negative thoughts. I always thought that people playing games of office politics were stupid people. But they're not. You learn about all the different kinds of perspectives people have and why they have them. Now I'm drawing diagrams all the time at work, 'Oh, that's a funny problem.' This is the most practical OU course of all for work.

How was the OU right for you?

Because it is so easy, as you change and develop, to make as many changes as you like in the way your studies go. There's no other university can make that happen. I mean, once you're on a course, you're on a course. To switch elsewhere is a big deal.

When I was in Fleet Street, working shifts, I always had a book when I was there at the weekends and evenings. I don't know how instrumental I've been, but loads of the people I used to work with at Fleet Street have carried on and done the OU. I must have been one of the very first people at Reuters to do it and it has flowered and a lot of people do it now. Now they make you pay for your first year and give you the money if you pass the exam. And then carry on sponsoring you after that.

I see that it was easy for you to balance your OU studies with your other responsibilities, but what about women with families?

My experience with men is they can be single-minded about what they want to do; anything they don't want to do, they don't do. And women aren't like that. All the time women do things they don't want to do like housework and cleaning, running around after people, basically being self-sacrificing. Any woman who has a career and kids, I have unbounded admiration for. I find it hard enough just looking after me and one tiny flat. It's the whole basis of society that men don't have to be caring and self-sacrificing. They think that they've got a right not to be. And once more, they're educated to believe in that right. And we're educated to believe in that right as well.

It's up to women to change it, but how, is one enormous problem. Men aren't going to change it voluntarily. Why should they? They've got all the advantages. Who gives up that kind of advantage and power voluntarily?

The reason I haven't married, although I've lived with several people, I never met a man that I felt I had the kind of respect for that you need to commit the rest of your life to. When you're young, you're looking to find somebody who is going to fill all the areas of your life and that is a pretty impossible dream. When I was young I had lots of boyfriends, there was the dancing boyfriend, the poetry-reading boyfriend, and the boy to go down to the pub with. I had more than one dancing one because I loved dancing. And then I met this one guy and we lived together for eight years. There was a point when I did want to marry him and he didn't want to marry me, and later he wanted to marry me and I didn't want to marry him because I knew that he wasn't going to develop in the same way I was going to.

What qualities do other women need to succeed in technology?

First of all, technology is getting to be less of a problem area for women to get into. Particularly in computing, it must be close to fifty-fifty. You need a belief in yourself more than anything else. You've got to say to yourself, 'I can do it.' You can't say, 'I can't.' Then there's an awful lot of help that you can get, tutors and counsellors are there and, of course, your fellow students. The courses that have been easier for me are the ones where I found women and we got together and talked. The hardest courses were the two programming courses, digital computer and one on databases. Those were more male-dominated so I didn't have as much to do with fellow students and they didn't have a summer school and there really were no self-helps.

My job as a project co-ordinator is a good job for a woman. It is a very feminine job, because, while there are technical aspects to it, it is trying to smooth the path and make people's working lives easier. You are trying to solve problems for people and also anticipate people's problems. I haven't met many women engineers, but they certainly want to work in teams. Men engineers, one, want to work on their own and not be part of a team, and two, divorce themselves of any kind of social implications of the work that they do. They're good at camaraderie among themselves, but not when it comes to a particular piece of work. Their attitude is, 'Keep knowledge to yourself because knowledge is power. The more that you know that he doesn't, the better it is for you.' Whereas women are willing to share what they know and try to benefit the group as a whole, rather than themselves as individuals.

What was the hardest part of OU study? And the easiest?

The hardest was doing things when you don't feel like doing anything, when you're tired. You just haul your bum in here and say, 'Do it.'

I don't think any of it was particularly easy. Some courses have an initial assignment which is marked but doesn't count. So that you can assess what kind of standard they're looking for. That can be quite useful, like on the science foundation course, they do that. One important thing is not to be scared about phoning your tutor up. That's what they're there for, and they'll tell you if they can't talk to you and say when they can. The worst experience I had with a tutor was on DT200 and in the end it was not that bad. You built up projects so you do one assignment which is the initial part of the project. And then you do a second assignment a few weeks later which builds on that, and then you do a final one which is the analysis of a questionnaire on a particular subject that you've picked right from the very start.

You need feedback from your tutor and mine had gone to Israel. But I created a fuss and got another tutor and luckily we were on the OU conference system so I sent my assignments electronically and he sent me his comments right back. On the whole they are very, very helpful people.

And I was always lucky with summer school. I always had someone to go with. If you've got a self-help group, one of the first things you should have on your agenda, is what kind of weeks you can make summer school, so that a couple of you can go together. It's so nice to walk in there, register, get rooms next to each other, and know that if you need somebody at midnight, there's somebody whose door you can knock on. Somebody to go to breakfast with in that big room, where you don't know where to sit. A lot of people are scared. I was.

I did four summer schools. This summer at York was brilliant, which is a nice place to go to anyway. Everybody says that there's something incredible about the OU system of summer schools and they're absolutely right. You get these 120 people at a particular week at a particular place. Split them up alphabetically into groups of 10 or 12, stick them in a room with a tutor, and by the end of the week you still have a bunch of 12 total strangers but who are a cohesive group of people who have worked together like a dream.

For the maths summer school, it's important to set your own agenda and not stick to theirs. Tania and I decided after the very first day that the timetable was crazy and you could go mad if you followed it. Rather than go to every single thing that's laid on, choose very carefully what it is you want to achieve at summer school and do the things that are necessary for you to achieve that, and the rest of the time relax. Otherwise you get people coming to breakfast terribly intense, poring over computer printout.

What are the advantages of an OU education?

From early on in my life I've wanted to have the power to choose what kind of life I was going to have, even though I've always despised money. And I also believe in working-class pride, that you shouldn't forget your roots. No matter where you came from, you shouldn't be ashamed of it. You can be working-class and in control of your life.

But the OU made me feel much more pluralist. It does it by presenting a wide variety of views and you meet people you would never, ever have met, for example, Enyd. We did the science foundation course together for totally different reasons. I had to do a second foundation course, but she was doing it because she liked geology and she thought she needed some physics if she was going to do more geology. She came flouncing into the first tutorial looking totally flustered, hair sticking out, plunking this huge bag down, 'Oh God, I can't do all this.' The first project in the science foundation course is you have to measure the moon. Work it out with lenses, make your own telescope, it's really awful. It's always cloudy, you can never see it. Enyd and I had immediate rapport and she lived fairly close, so we had our little study group for the year and went to summer school together. But the point is she was a senior social worker in Tower Hamlets, her whole work experience was totally different from mine. And she's Welsh, plays tennis in this little Welsh tennis club. She dropped out the next year when she got a much more high-powered management job, doing a project on the implementation of the Children Act. But without the OU, I would never have got to know her.

Tell me about your career plans.

The thing is, I enjoy what I do at the moment, and because I've had quite a lot of changes in the recent past, I haven't got any big motivation for changing. I've had some ideas about an educational role outside. I would quite like to teach teenage kids. But not in a big school with disciplinary problems. It's the kind of thing that your eye might go to in the newspaper, although you're not looking for job opportunities. But if the page happens to open up, and you scan it, you might find the right kind of thing. You know that kind of unconscious process that then leads to other things? I don't know if your life's been like that, but mine's always been like that. My decision-making processes have never been terribly to the fore. I do sometimes sit down and think, Right, you've got to make a decision about this. But much more often the opportunity's there, and I take it. That's how things happen with me, mostly.

Chapter 7

Ellen Davies   *From DHSS Inspector to Dentist*

It's a bit of a closed shop in Britain, especially when that exam comes so early in life. I remember my mother kept on and on about the 11-plus. You have to pass it, that is the thing. You're given goals as children and you think automatically, I'm scared, I know I can't. In this country everything is cut and dried, unless you know as a very young child what you want to do on the academic side. It's very difficult to go on, later in life, and be something that is *you*.

The Open University publicity department described Ellen to the local and national media in January 1992 as follows:

> Mrs Ellen Davies, 38 (born 1953), Bridgend, Mid-Glamorgan, is a dentist who left school with seven O-levels and no specific career plan. She joined the Civil Service and ultimately became a DHSS inspector visiting companies about National Insurance.

Cliff and I were waiting at the rail station in Bridgend, when Ellen arrived breathless, declaring that she always misjudges how long it's going to take her to do this or that. Ellen is of medium height, wears no make-up, and has fluffy brown hair, big blue eyes and a wide grin. She wore an oversize blue shirt and lavender sweatpants. We did the interview in her living-room, where green plants spread their tendrils in all directions, a 16-year-old grey striped cat named Toby dozed beside us, and rare African clawed toads hid under their rocks in her aquarium.

Ellen speaks with a very muted and soft voice that is at the same time rapid-fire and extremely Welsh. 'I don't think I sounded Welsh when I was in Bristol, but now that I've come back to Wales, I think I sound very Welsh.' Yes, I thought so too.

Ellen started studying with the OU in 1980 after being divorced because she needed to 'join something that would make me stick to a timetable'. In 1984, with four and a half OU course credits behind her, she applied for a place as a dental student at Bristol University.

She started her dental course in October 1986 at short notice when a place suddenly became free, leaving her 13 days 'to resign from my job, do the ironing and find somewhere to live in Bristol'. The oldest of some nine mature students in her class, she now works in a dental practice at Kenfig Hill near Bridgend. While at university her hobby was hot-air ballooning.

What were your reasons for enrolling in the OU?

I got married in 1974, and he immediately lost his job and was virtually unemployed all the time we were married. When he left in 1978, I was really upset. I missed him tremendously even though I knew that at least things would now be stable. I lost a lot of weight, things really did seem black. I thought, I've got to join something. It was awful being on my own, the house was so quiet, so lonely.

At the same time people were knocking on the door because he'd run up thousands of pounds of debts and I was responsible for all his debts. So I had no money. But I've always liked gardening so I thought, I'll get an allotment and I can grow things and save money that way. I put my name down on the council list and got an allotment six months later. I also put my name down for the Open University. I didn't know anybody who had done it. I learned about it because after an OU television programme, a little bit of advertising comes up. I phoned up and got all the information and then you get this letter back which says you can join in a year's time and I thought, But I want to do it now!

The first year after my divorce was awful because there are so many things you have to get used to on your own. But in life, if nothing happens and you don't have any problems, you don't really change much, do you? And when bad things happen, good things can also happen.

I started with S101, the science foundation course. I looked at the first couple of units and saw we had to measure how far it is to the moon. I thought, Oh, no. So I took the units down to my Uncle Bob. And he said, 'Oh, this is very straightforward.' But I thought, How can I do it? Work with all these equations? We had weekly tutorial groups in Bridgend and I made two lovely friends. The tutors were so informative, kind, understanding and enthusiastic. As for the cost, you pay a small amount and then another amount in April, and all of us were thinking, I'll give it up in April, and not pay the rest, not carry on with it. Because it was a new thing entirely. It was a lot of work at the beginning. We had to sit down, read these books, watch the television. The computer-marked assignments were okay, but the essays, you worried about. Every time the OU homework came back, the postman wouldn't put it through the door, he'd knock on the door and say, 'It's come back, did you get a good grade?'

What obstacles or constraints did you have to succeeding with the OU?

Up until the 11-plus, I'd always come top in class, so my teachers couldn't believe I didn't pass it. But if you haven't got much confidence, you don't look at yourself as a person. And the 11-plus was a big thing. You had to do it. You had to pass it. Out of the blue this thing has to be done. And oh gosh, I can't do it. When I got to the exam I just panicked.

I stayed on in this Catholic school and did another year. Then at the girls' grammar school, they had more seats than children and they thought they should have passed more children. So I got transferred there in the second year. But in the grammar school, depending on how well you did in your first year, what your best subjects were, you got streamed in the second year into Latin or Arts. If you were in the Latin stream you did the pure sciences, physics, chemistry, and biology. If you were in the Arts stream, you got French and general science. They put me in the Arts stream and you can't do an A-level in general science. My seven O-levels were in maths, general science, English language and literature, cookery, needlework and art.

In contrast to me, I've got a brother who's got no inferiority complex. Just does what he enjoys and does it well. My parents put him in a private school where you can get a good education but you have to pay to go there. Then they moved him up to Summerhill, another private school. He got shunted from pillar to post for his education's sake and he ended up getting just two O-levels.

Anyway, when I passed my O-levels at 16, I had no idea what I wanted to do. There was nothing I could combine maths with to go on into the A-levels. I also didn't know what specific jobs I might like.

My low expectations have always been an obstacle, but there are also the expectations of other people, or the lack of expectations. When I started doing the OU, a lot of people said, 'What are you doing that for? Who do you think you are?' A bit like you had delusions of grandeur, or you weren't satisfied with life as it was with them.

This came out much more when I wanted to go to college. I hadn't told my mother I was applying, but I rang her up when I got admitted. It knocked her for six. I had a job and was settled and now I was thinking of throwing it away and doing something else? Although my parents had wanted more education for me when I was younger, it was a shock for me to do it now in this strange way. In fact, my Dad, when I joined the OU, said, 'Well, I don't think you'll be able to do this.' So when I told my mother I was going to dental college, she said, 'Do you know what you're doing?' I said, 'I'm sure.' She rang back half an hour later and said, 'I'm sorry, I didn't mean to sound like that. Does this mean you're going to be a dentist?'

How has the OU been important in your life?

Back in 1982 I thought, I'm getting older and unless I do something, I'm never going to be trained to do anything else. And with the OU you go from thinking, 'Can I pass my first exam? Could I take a second class? Should I drop this? Shall I carry on until summer school?' to the stage where you do the OU and it is lovely. You feel so capable, you say, 'If I can do this, I can go to college. Well, after all, children do it, 18-year-old children go to university. If they can do it, why can't I?'

By 1983 I still had the allotment and was doing lots of things, camping, sailing. Every single time I sailed over to Ilfracombe I'd always take my OU units along with me, but the OU was beginning to take second place with me. Despite the fact that the OU was the best type of learning for me. You've got to do your TMAs and your CMAs (computer-marked assignments) every fortnight, so you can't get that far behind. If I'm left on my own, I do nothing till the end and then try to cram it all in. But the OU wouldn't let me leave it for weeks. So the OU gave me confidence. And even though I had a nice job in the civil service, I had no specific qualification. In thirty years' time, I thought, will I be doing exactly the same job? Or my boss's job? And the answer to that was, No.

What impacts has the OU had on your career?

If I hadn't done OU I'd never have dreamed that I could go to college, ever. Gradually you think, I can do this and I have enough confidence now to resign my job and go to college. You can step out.

When I was debating about college, I got moved from the Inspectorate to Fraud, another mobile job, checking up that people were working, watching people. I didn't really like it. I wanted something that deals with people and is practical and professional. And dentistry was the only thing I thought I could do. But the first college I inquired at, she said 'How old are you? Good God, you'll be nearly 38 by the time you've qualified. We can't have that. You are far too old.' I thought, Oh, dear, is that true? Perhaps I have left it far too late.

And so in June of '86 I rang Bristol up and sent off my CV and got an encouraging letter back that said obviously I wouldn't be able to get in for 1986, but to apply through UCCA (for normal students' entrance into university) in September '86 for October '87. It was such a lovely letter I rang them up in August hoping that somebody hadn't got the A-level grades they needed. On September 19, I had a letter back saying for me to come along. I was over the moon. So I filled out an application form and was accepted.

What's been the most important use you've made of your OU degree?

It got me into dental school, didn't it? Talk about culture shock. All my life I've had friends of all ages, twenties, thirties, forties, fifties and my friends have always had friends of all ages. And you go to college and they're all 18 and they've never had friends in other age groups.

Also they've all done A-levels. So it was, 'Didn't you do that in A-levels? Oh, we did that in A-levels.' They had done biology, physics and chemistry, the pure sciences. I felt like a fish out of water, an aged crone in this sea of young wonders. I was renting a flat in an old rectory with a family that had a couple of children. The first year is very busy, you do a lot of lecture time. They placed five dental students in each hall of residence and so after lectures from nine to five, the regular students went back and studied in groups of five. And the mature students went back to their lonely flats. But the OU had taught me how to study on my own.

The first year was all academic, it was lectures every single day, biochemistry, physiology and anatomy. It was very different from the OU. The OU gives you all the facts and it gives you what you need to know to do your homework and pass the exams. Dental college gives you the facts but it's up to you to make sense of them and remember them. We had exams at Christmas in which I didn't do very well. And more exams in the summer. It was a struggle, but I got through to the second year. Such a difference. It was practical. You learn about all sorts of decay, the instruments you use, the materials you use. I enjoyed it a lot and by this time the social milieu was nice because we were all together.

Then in January 1988 we started clinical duties in small groups. Orthodontics, surgery, X-ray. And the academic side, again lectures, in pharmacology, human diseases, but it was all much more meaningful now.

In the junior and senior years you had your own patients and you were in the same group of students and rotated into different departments in dentistry. It lasted four and a half years. I finished in December 1990.

There were nine mature students in the group of 44, half were men, half women, but our teachers were definitely men. They say that women tend to go into the community side of dentistry and are salaried, but all of the women I know, whether older women who qualified a few years back, or students who qualified the same year as me, have gone into traditional family practice dentistry.

Most people going to university get a grant. But if you have got a degree already, you wouldn't get the grant. So if I had carried on and got my degree with the OU, I wouldn't then have been able to get a grant for college. So that was very fortunate that I had stopped. If I had got my degree and wanted to go to college, that would have really made it difficult for me financially.

How did you study for your OU courses? What was your routine?

You have TMAs and CMAs to do at regular intervals and you've got to keep your reading up to date. I made a point of studying one or two evenings a week on weeknights. I'd come home, feed the cat, have tea, if I had clothes to wash, I'd wash them, then I'd settle down for two hours. And then go to bed. I definitely made a point of two evenings a week and then all Saturday afternoon or all Sunday morning.

As a beginner, I was really nervous about the essays. I'd never written any essays since I was 13 years old. I'd need to write them out three times in the beginning.

I liked geology best at the OU. When I was taking my OU courses, I also went to geology lectures on Tuesday nights at Bristol University and I joined the geology field trips with students from Bristol University. They'd pick me up on the motorway, and I also did a summer two-week geology research class with them. OU summer schools in geology are in Durham because it has a good department and there's a lot of geology in Durham. If I take more courses, they will be geology because I'd like to be a summer school OU tutor.

Why would you advise women today to do an OU degree?

Whether you want to get a degree, or a lot of experience or qualification in a certain area, or you want to do it out of interest, it is a springboard for other things. I think everyone should do it. What do people do with their time? They do exercise, they watch television, they go to the pub, go to the theatre, but most things don't entail much learning. And once you've left school and you've got a mortgage or a family or commitments, you can't step back into school again. You've left that. So the OU is an absolute lifeline.

As far as employers go, I think an OU qualification or degree is definitely regarded as worth something, although they view it differently from a conventional degree. By definition, the people tend to be older, they've done it all off their own bat, and they've got the qualification. So it took a lot more decision-making on the part of that individual than for someone who's gone through the regular education system.

Tell me some more about the impact of the OU on your self-confidence.

I'd think, I've got this homework, but I'd do all sorts of things to put it off, like wander out into the rockery. I'm scared to begin things because I know I've got to concentrate and I might not understand it. Practical things, fine, I can understand them, but what you do academically reflects your brain, doesn't it? And you're a bit scared to show off how useless your brain is. But the OU helps you with this by presenting each subject in such an understandable way; they really take you through it.

The OU gives you confidence that you can take things in, you can manage things, you can pass the exam at the end of the year. It started off, that first exam, I was shaking like mad when I took it. The second year I wasn't so scared, and by year three, you just go in and do *your* exam.

What was the hardest part of OU study? The easiest?

For summer school I went to Nottingham. There were four topics, physics, earth sciences, biology and chemistry. In the summer school you had to do three practical sessions. And depending on the coloured spot you got, you either did biology or physics or whatever. I had a red spot, which meant I was doing physics, and I was so scared about physics I swapped my spot with somebody else who wasn't doing physics. And when it came back, it's always the same in life, physics was the best thing of all. In the science summer school we had evening tutorials to go to and the physics ones were absolutely brilliant. They were packed, with standing ovations at the end. And I said, 'I wish I'd done physics. Why did I back out?'

I chose maths M101 next because I thought that would do me good. I'd never been able to understand maths. So when I was done with it, I wanted to go on with something far more interesting to me. I did a half-credit geology course and S202 Biology, Form and Functioning after that, and then went back into geology. So I had four and a half credits in 1984 and I took 1985 off and then applied to dental college.

If you had it to do over again, would you do your OU education differently?

I wasn't doing OU for good grades or for the purpose of getting into college. I was doing it for further knowledge. But having gone to university now, my attitude has changed. You can really see the value of what *you* do. For my OU courses, at the end of each unit was a recommended reading list. Well, I never read a word of a recommended reading list. Now I can see there's a lot more to studying. When you go to an everyday university, it's up to you what you get out of it, the enjoyment you can get out of it. I know that if I treat a course as something that I've *got* to do, and not put my heart and soul into it, I won't do very well at the end of the day.

The years I did OU and didn't put myself into it, I think what a waste! All the effort that the OU puts into a really good course. Everything was on a plate for me. And I just skimmed through it. At this late stage, though, life's what you make it and the more you bother, the better it is.

What are your career plans?

I really like geology, but when it comes to jobs, very few people who qualify in geology get jobs in geology. They go into something like advertising. The height of petroleum exploration was in the 1970s, and the only other geology jobs are in teaching. I wouldn't have been any good as a lecturer. So when I thought about college, I wanted to be trained in something that I could go out and find a job in easily, straight away.

I like dentistry, but it is a job. And I love my spare time. Just after I left university, I thought, I do love dentistry. But at the same time, what else can I do? Shall I be a vet? Because I've done eleven years of studying and you get hooked. And while I love the job I'm doing, the majority of jobs, after three or four years, become the same old job and the OU made me realize there are many other things in life that I can get involved in.

I definitely want to take more OU courses and get an honours degree. I want to do evolution, oceanography, more geology.

What was most important in your life before and after the OU?

Before what I was pivoting my life around was my husband. I wanted to be married and happy and he was the controlling factor 24 hours a day. I was 21 when I got married and I'd never actually seen myself as an individual at all.

Before the OU, all I ever thought I should be was a good and proper person. You behaved yourself. You had your job. You went to work at 9 o'clock, you came home at 5 o'clock. That was it. That isn't it. There are loads of things that can just crop up and happen that you can do. And you don't ever want to say no.

Now I like everything I'm doing. My life is settled in that I can manage, I'm qualified, I've got a job. There's no uncertainty. When I came back here I missed the student things I used to do, so I joined mountain rescue. I'm really happy. But I know from past experience, it's not going to go on exactly like this for 10 or 20 years.

Our visit with Ellen ended with lunch at the Wyndham Hotel in Bridgend's town centre. Her most recent enthusiasm is the Bridgend Mountain Rescue Team. When she wrote to them, they inquired back, did she know another woman who wanted to come along as well? Until then it hadn't dawned on her that it would be an all-male team. Mountain rescue is just the kind of hobby that appeals to Ellen. It's practical, it deals with people, and it combines knowledge and skills. But I wouldn't want to bet on where her future interests will lead her!

Chapter 8

Channelling

Enid Castle is principal of Cheltenham Ladies' College. 'A single-sex college has the benefit of providing for girls; there is no sense that some subjects are better for girls than boys.' Lisa Jardine is professor of English at London's Queen Mary College. 'I am committed to girls' schools because they don't inhibit specializing in science, as my daughter and I did.' Elizabeth Wilson is a writer and academic. 'It does seem single-sex education is better for girls' intellectual advancement. In particular, it's vital to have single-sex teaching in "boys" subjects – maths and science – even if the school is co-ed.' (*Guardian 2*, 8 September 1993, p. 9)

'Girls widen school lead over boys and catch up at colleges,' reads a 1992 *Guardian* headline. Between 1976 and 1989, boys leaving school with an O-level or its equivalent rose from 49 per cent to 60 per cent. But girls went from 52 per cent to 67 per cent! And in 1990 women students occupied 47 per cent of places on first degree courses, compared with 41 per cent in 1980.

Cause for celebration? Certainly. However, what about this same article saying that girls did markedly better in English, biology, French and history, and boys better in chemistry, physics, geography and maths?

In spite of the gains women are making in education, channelling is still with us. Channelling refers to the fact that girls enroll more than boys in traditionally 'female' subjects, and boys enroll more than girls in traditionally 'male' subjects. Channelling is also responsible for girls outperforming boys in traditionally 'female' subjects and doing worse than boys in traditionally 'male' subjects.

How are little girls channelled?

Girls get channelled by their earliest teachers through example. In 1988–89, the proportion of men teaching at the primary level was 19 per cent, while at university level it was 87 per cent (Department of Education and Science, 1991, p. xi). And it's going to stay that way: 77 per cent of education students in 1989–90 were women (Universities' Statistical Record, 1991, p. 16). Mums and primary teachers – this is what girls see women doing.

Girls also get channelled by such a background detail as dinner ladies. I asked myself,

'What's a grown woman doing at the end of a skipping rope in a school playground?' (*Guardian* photo of 3 February 1992). She is a dinner lady teaching the girls to play the games she used to play. Why are there no dinner men in the picture, teaching the boys *and* the girls the games *they* used to play?

Another way girls get channelled is by schools' honouring girls' success in 'women's subjects' and ignoring their success in 'men's subjects'.

> To be assured of high academic honour within the school the subjects to excel at were English literature and history. Being good at science and mathematics had no great social cachet or appeal. Like almost every girls' grammar or public school of its time, the school attached academic importance firmly and squarely to traditional arts subjects and failed to encourage or develop skills of numeracy and experimentation. (Evans, 1991, p. 13)

And remember from Dale Godfrey's chapter how Father Christmas is still giving little boys magnets and little girls beads? It all adds up.

How are young women channelled?

Teenagers get channelled by *not* having the sex-stereotyped attitudes they bring with them challenged by teachers. Michael Davis, head of science at a mixed-sex high school in Manchester, says that up to the age of 13 girls are definitely equal in ability to the boys. But at 13, when pupils choose what they will take, girls don't choose science. Why? Dr Jan Harding, an educational researcher, says girls believe science is only appropriate for boys because girls are going to be homemakers, not breadwinners (Lowe, 1992).

For those teenagers who buck the tide and *do* take traditionally 'masculine' subjects, there are sexist teachers to channel them back to the straight and narrow. John Pratt (1985) in a national survey found half of men teachers opposed to equal opportunities. Teachers agreed (72 per cent): teachers tend to give pupils the impression that some subjects are more appropriate for one sex than the other! Teachers of physical sciences and crafts showed the least sympathy to equal opportunities, but there was also strong opposition among teachers of maths and PE, which are core subjects even if they do carry traces of masculinity.

And as for today's curriculum, Jim Sweetman (1992), a GCSE chief examiner, says, 'It is probable that the central characters in the set books will be men, that the international conflicts in the 20th century studied in history will have been started by men, and that the same number of men will still be digging the same hole in the road at the same speed as they did 30 years ago.' At the end of these courses, young women face male chief examiners, mostly male examining teams, and exams devised for male test takers.

How serious is the channelling obstacle today?

Consider this. Teacher trainees were asked to comment on a school report. It was always the same report, but for half of the trainees it was Jane Smith's, and for half, it was John Smith's. The trainees' conclusions regarding Jane's performance were that she was weak in maths and science, strong in literary subjects, and would make a good secretary. On the other hand, they concluded that John could use some help in maths and science, but he would make a good Civil Service manager because he seemed to be good at everything.

Under such circumstances, says Dale Spender (1984), 'the chances of implementing equality of educational opportunity are remote – and unrealistic'.

Surely, 1990s pupils aren't behaving according to old stereotypes. Yes, they are, says Her Majesty's Inspectorate (Department for Education, 1992). In a survey of eight schools, they found unfortunate imbalances in pupils' subject choices at 13+, in line with sex-role stereotypes. Child development was the total preserve of the girls, information technology the preserve of the boys. At one school visited by HMI, the teachers believed girls were inferior to boys in mathematics and physics abilities, and this had become a self-fulfilling prophecy in the choices of A-level subjects by girls.

As recently as 1988–89, the percentages of pupils leaving school with O-level grades A to C and CSE grade 1 were: English, girls 52%, boys 38%; French, girls 23%, boys 14%; physics, girls 10%, boys 23%. The courses where the greatest sex differences are found remain technology (metal, wood, etc.), with girls 9% and boys 23%, and business and domestic courses, with girls 24% and boys 6% (Department of Education and Science, 1991, p. 38).

There was also a big sex difference in pupils leaving school with *two or more* GCE A-levels: 48 per cent of girls had passed exams in English/arts/social studies versus 26 per cent of boys; 48 per cent of boys had passed exams in mathematics/science versus 30 per cent of girls.

Young women may be going farther these days, but in the same old, predictable directions.

Who better to tell you about channelling than Open University honours graduate, Frances Smith, the subject of the next chapter. Frances wanted to be a botanist, but when it came to A-levels she was told she had two choices: English, French and Latin, or English, history and Latin. Neither made any sense for a would-be scientist, so she left school.

Chapter 9

Frances Smith *From Jobbing Gardener to Specialist Salad Grower*

At my first summer school I wrote 'Frances Smith' on my name badge in the same size, neat letters filling the space. Then I noticed a chap whose badge read 'JIM' with his surname barely visible below. Another 'ah-ha' experience. At every summer school after that I put my Christian name in large letters right across the middle of the badge and my surname very small underneath. Because the OU is a first-name organization. This is very difficult for people to accept who have been used to only surnames in school. And I didn't like it very well – until I discovered who this new 'Frances' was.

Frances and her husband Neil own Park Hill Produce & Appledore Salads, reached by the little rattling Marsh Link railway from Ashford. Neil picked up Cliff and me hiking along the road from the station and drove us to the farmhouse where Frances met us at the back door with a soup pan in her hand. She was wearing farmer togs, faded red trousers and sweatshirt. She is stocky, has shoulder-length straight brown hair, a pretty, smooth, pink face, and hands and nails stained with black earth.

She had sent the following terse description of herself in the winter of 1991:

> Age 48, married 26 years, 2 children 23, 21. From 1977, S100, T101, and onwards to first-class honours in 1984 in science subjects over 8 years. Now growing specialist salads and veg for chefs; husband breeds quail. Have much to thank OU for in building confidence in communication skills, so now quite fearless on local TV, radio, etc. Last year got on TV in Master Chef Cooking Competition.

The four of us had lunch at the small, square table where Frances used to do her OU TMAs. It was a cold, grey November day and the house, with brickwork from 1830 and a foundation from Anglo-Saxon times, was chilly. This room, which used to be a Victorian kitchen, had blackened beams so low that Cliff could stand up straight only in between them. The house is surrounded by 23 acres of gardens, poly tunnels, quail sheds, and grazing land for sheep.

When our husbands disappeared, Frances shoved the bread-board, dirty dishes, water glasses, and newspapers to the other side of the table and I pushed my tape recorder button. But she immediately sprang up and raced off to get laminated photocopies of her OU course transcript and bachelor's diploma. Her transcript lists 14 courses, most done with distinction.

She also produced a paperback book she had appeared in, *Master Chefs 1990*, containing winning recipes from BBC's amateur chef competition. Frances was among three from the Southeast who had proudly prepared a dinner menu for the judges. The book said that Park Hill grows 300 different plants and raises quail and guinea-fowl, and that Frances' inspiration was her mother, who during post-war rationing could improvise a meal out of nothing.

Why did you pursue an OU degree?

In 1976 Neil lost his job in the City and, like me, he hadn't been to university, so he was at a disadvantage competing with graduates. It was he who initially wrote off for the bumpf and he who decided, first, to do an OU degree on the social sciences side, economics. I looked over the OU materials and knew it wouldn't work because, being the sort of person I am, I knew I'd be sticking my nose into it, so I said, 'I'd better do my own.' And I decided no way was I doing arts because that's what I'd been brought up with. I'd had arts up to here. I also had this magnet for science. So I wrote off to do S100 and, crushing disappointment, no room for either of us the first year. So it was 1977 when we both started an Open University degree.

My first goal was not a degree but simply to finish the course I was most interested in, genetics. Only then did I set my sights on a degree. Only then did I tell my parents and friends what I'd been up to for the past three years. Only after genetics would I know if I had the academic capability to do better than a third. My father had dinned it into me that if I had a first-class brain, why didn't it show? And I'd respond, 'Because *you* wouldn't let me do science.' Now I had to prove myself right. My father read my OU essays and said they didn't sound like me at all. To which I replied, 'Of course, it doesn't sound like the me that *you* think I am. This sounds like the me that you didn't know was there.'

In any case, we had been here since 1971 when Candida was four and Julian two because Neil decided to bring up the family as country children. I had decided to be a wife until the children had got their O-levels, at which point I was going to review the situation. But Neil found another job as an investment analyst in the City and it stopped him from doing his OU degree. Of course, I didn't find a job in stocks and so I went on. Eventually Neil became unhappy with his work and in the middle of my degree course, we bought our first three quail. My vegetable and salad business didn't start until 1984 at the end of my OU course work, at the suggestion of one of the chefs who came to buy quail.

What obstacles or constraints did you have on studying for a degree?

I sat O-levels in eight subjects, but didn't do A-levels. And why I didn't do A-levels is very relevant to why I did Open University. To start with, my father was educated at Rugby and got a first-class degree in history from Oxford. My mother was educated by governesses at home and worked as a journalist from 16 to 60. My school, St Paul's Girls School, was a very fine academic girls' school modelled on its boys' school partner, St Paul's Boys School. The organization of study was based on a system where at 14 you had to make a decision. You had to choose whether you were going to do sciences, languages or classics. And if you were going to do sciences, whether you were going to take physics, or not. Now I wanted to take biology because I was not particularly interested in physics and chemistry at that time. But biology was regarded as the option for the stupid, who were not clever enough to tackle either Greek (classics), German (modern languages), or physics with chemistry. I could have done the physics with chemistry, but, although I was in the first division for maths, they said that my maths was not good enough!

So biology was one of my O-level subjects and I did very well in it, but it was the only science on my O-level list. But when it came to A-levels, the school didn't like my choices at all. I wanted to be a botanist and decided that the most rational combination of subjects for a botanist were zoology, French, English, and Latin as a nonexaminable subject. But the school said, 'No, you will do either English, French and Latin, or English, history and Latin.' So I sulkily did the former for a term and a half and then rebelled. I no longer had any clear objective for university.

In my mind the whole thing was a disaster. How could I go to university and study botany on the basis of English, French and Latin? So I left school and my father's solution – he had trained as a barrister before the war – was for this stroppy 17-year-old to have a go at the law.

So I started to read for the bar in 1960. My father found me a tutor, although the tutorial system didn't suit me, but I did try to please my parents because they thought I had behaved so badly. However, my serious studying only lasted until I did the season. Dances and parties became important, I fell in love, and got thoroughly fed up with the law. Finally my tutor rang my father and said he wouldn't go on, I was too young, and I was wasting his time and my father's money.

Any current-day obstacles?
We were so strapped for cash in 1981 I rang up the Labour Exchange and began working as a jobbing gardener three days a week in Rye to pay my OU fees. I tended people's front and back gardens, keeping them tidy, pruning, digging, hoeing, weeding, all the things I did in my own garden.

So coming up with the cash was a problem and physically getting away from the house for tutorials was a problem, as was arranging summer schools and for Neil to look after the children. My day schools were in Guildford and my tutorials in Tunbridge Wells and Broadstairs. Then, summer is the busiest time of the year for anyone living a smallholding type life, which meant summer schools, while wonderful, were very inconvenient.

Also, the OU is like a rare disease that you can't talk about except to somebody who's shared the experience. The OU is deeply boring to people who haven't done it. I couldn't, and can't now, talk to my own family – because they haven't done it and they don't understand it. My friends who are just starting foundation courses find the same thing. They can talk among themselves, but if 'outsiders' are there, these people feel shut out of OU conversations.

What does the OU mean to you?
It meant to me the chance to study all the subjects that had been effectively barred to me all my life because I just hadn't had the opportunity to look at them properly. I'd always been very interested in science, but my parents didn't understand science at all and don't want to. So it was an opening for me to find out whether what I had thought was going to be so exciting, was. It was every bit as exciting as I thought it would be, and more, and just to find out about the tangible world, inside out and outside in, out to the stars and back, and to have it all there together was so deeply satisfying, it was amazing. It allowed me to

find out if the me I thought was there inside me really was. And to find that it was there, I never would have done without the Open University. My husband rescued me from my parents. And the Open University rescued me from the whole set-up. I could start again. Give myself the education I should have had.

Gardening had always been my hobby and I made my first garden at age 16 on a rooftop in London together with my mother. It was she who nurtured my interest in botany like crazy, starting in the car-parks of country pubs. Daddy would drive us out on weekends and when he went into the pub for a beer, Mum would get out the books on British flora. Mother always had an educated interest in animals, birds, flowers, nature, in an artistic, airy-fairy way. It was fun to find out the names of things. It was a very good occupation for a mother and daughter.

How has the OU changed you?

I've always been interested in 'How come?' I was the elephant's child for questions never satisfactorily answered. And I believed that if I could just once get there, I would be able to find out *how* to find out the answers to any questions that I wanted to ask. And I now know where to find the answer to any question I ask. I may choose not to ask it, but at least I am totally certain I can go and explore anything. It's this precious tool of being able to go find out, that I never had. I knew a little bit about how a scientific experiment was conducted, but I'd never actually done one. And now I have. And I know how to do another. I can set up an experiment on any subject within my competence. I would know how to do it, I would know how to analyse it, and I would know whether it meant anything or not. The OU has opened up every possibility.

What's the most important use you make of your degree?

Not a day goes by when I don't use something, whether it was a fact or an attitude or an approach or a habit. I use it all, the simple biology, geology, soil science, genetics and physiology to enhance the productivity of the various ecosystems running at Park Hill. Genetics in particular has earned its weight in gold. It prevented me from making disastrous mistakes.

You know how you exclaimed over the chicks, that some were yellow? Well, there is a strong desire in people who keep stock to improve what they produce. In the case of quail a breeder might want bigger birds or birds that lay lots of eggs or birds that mature quickly. But suppose you had the idea that chefs would pay more for blonde-coloured birds and so you decided you'd breed for blonde skin. Where the genetics comes in is that this particular project is genetically impossible. Blonde males are not very fertile and blonde females are not keen on laying eggs. So your first generation might be absolutely fine, but the next generation simply wouldn't perform. Because if you knew genetics, you'd know that blondes already were a minority and you would be trying to broaden a gene base which was far too narrow and, hence, you are going to get inbreeding depression and how! And you'll see it in two generations. And then you might do all sorts of things to get them to perform, but in fact, you had bred them *not* to perform.

What I've done is strike a balance between birds that do all the things they are supposed to do, which is to lay eggs and grow to a saleable size in a reasonable time with a reasonable feed-conversion factor. And I have sustained this for ten years without bringing in any new blood. In fact, we don't want somebody else's new cocks at Park Hill because our birds are required to produce their own natural resistance to common ailments. They don't get medicated feed. The weak die, the robust make it.

What do you mean by using an attitude?

Using two valuable 'lessons' learnt. First, the importance of listening to everyone's opinion before forming a judgement and that no one person is any more 'right' than any other. And the second 'lesson' is that this also applies to oneself, so one is equally entitled to be heard.

I remember an OU tutor who asked a mousy little girl in the corner what her opinion was. And how a very pushy laboratory technician, who was always monopolizing the discussion, spoke up before the young woman could open her mouth and said, 'What I think is', and went through his piece again. And the tutor said, 'Just a minute. Do remember that everybody's opinion is just as valuable as everybody else's. I would like to hear what she thinks.' The woman went absolutely purple but produced a perfectly reasonable argument, after which the tutor said, 'Right. Now we'll go right around and hear everybody's opinion.' And we did and I thought, Gosh, that's quite something. I must remember that.

So I've turned it on its head at home as well, a recent instance being taking on our church organist in Parochial Church Council meetings. Our organist wants a modern hymn sung from our new book at every service, but I have argued for singing old-fashioned hymns at old-fashioned services and modern hymns at modern services, because I know that some of the older members of the congregation are unhappy with the new music. And if my opinion is as valuable as everybody else's, then I mustn't be browbeaten. But without the OU, I would never have dreamed of arguing with the organist. And as a result of this outspokenness, *not* an endearing and feminine quality, I have been given the post of Churchwarden and I shall need all the skills I can muster, as we are having a turbulent phase of village politics right now.

How did you balance your OU studies with your family responsibilities?

I got my degree in ten minuteses, meaning there were units all over the house, a book in every room, and if I had 10 minutes, I would read a page of a unit. Assignments were written at night after everyone had gone to bed and the dishwasher was thundering away. I could study no matter how noisy it was. Working against distraction was not a problem. London day-school pupils learn to ignore other children screaming at play outside, or the party their parents are giving downstairs.

I had a CMA mate for each course I took. We would phone each other up and take it in turn to say what answer we'd got to a problem and would only discuss it if we disagreed. My tutors always handed out a list of everybody who agreed to have their names and addresses released. The tutors' attitude was that they were there to facilitate, but that what we did was up to us.

What other advice would you have for other women doing the OU?

I did a summer school every year. They are essential for science courses. There is always a question on the exam based on summer school so you won't get that if you don't attend. You store up trouble if you miss summer school and the opportunity to sort out the blips in your learning curve. There's always something you can't get the hang of.

When I went to the S100 summer school I went to the course counselling. I am a great believer in going to those counselling sessions. No reason not to. You might learn something. And I came across Mary Bell, a regional course counsellor, and she had me sussed. She said, 'I know what you're after.' And I think she did, too. She's a very skilled counsellor. Very nice person. 'You go for that genetics and as soon as you've started it, come see me and we'll talk about the rest of your degree. It's a very good target and when you think you're going to hit it, time to look for a new one.' And that's what I did. I took the targets one at a time.

In fact, I didn't see Mary Bell again, but after genetics, every year I saw a counsellor to plan out the next step in my degree. From 1981 to 1984 I took six third-level courses: Evolution, Physiology, Biochemistry, Ecology, Oceanography, and Surface and Sedimentary Processes. I would have been happy with grades at level 2, but it was very nice that my exam results pulled my marks over the border so that I earned a first-class honours degree. I feel I am a natural scientist. My studies were hardly a major struggle, rather a joy all the way.

What quality in you was most responsible for your success with the OU?

I'm a fast reader, I'm very good with words, I can string ideas together. I can take a whole load of data and after a suitable period of time of it sloshing around in my skull, I can either put it into order or I'll be off to find out where I've gone wrong. I have a brain that likes to play with things inside itself and it was starved of material before I did my OU degree. I would read the papers with attention, hoping there would be something interesting in them. There never was. I needed things to think about.

So as soon as the S100 materials arrived I was completely enthralled. I was grabbed. It was like a new religion. I suddenly realized that here was what I'd been looking for. Here was the opportunity. And there was that one subject that had been pecking away. Only children often are very interested in genetics and, of course, you've got all these ancestors coming down to a single individual. I looked at the courses that were available and the prerequisites and decided I would do whatever I had to, to do that course, and do it successfully.

Tell me about your career plans.

My plan is to get the veg business on a paying basis. In its third year as a full-time operation it turns over £50,000 annually. I feel it's nearly right and the thing to do is not make the mistakes I've made again. You can grow too much of something that doesn't sell. And run out of something that does sell. You can charge too little or charge too much. You can have crop failures, or you can raise very good Cape gooseberries in the tunnels, but when they come in from Colombia at 99p for a big box, it doesn't matter what a success your gooseberries are.

We have acquired quite a reputation as one of the more innovative growers of leaves for restaurants. It's the only way you can generally describe everything that runs from a herb through to a carrot, really, they're all leaves. Some chefs call leaves lettuces. I just call the whole lot leaves because that way you cover the orientals, the Europeans, the Americans, the standard leaves, the wild leaves (we grow wild sorrel, wild cress). We grow them and pick them and they go off in the lorry along with apples and potatoes, which we buy in, to 35 different customers each week, in London and the Southeast. And we are proud to be able to supply restaurants with Michelin stars stuff they really like. Some are quite particular but they keep my standards up. There's a chef in Tunbridge Wells who has made me grow all the queer gear, which is what the trade calls any leaf other than a lettuce. So I'm a queer gear specialist. So what would be nice would be if the business made some money, but growing conditions get more and more difficult and, of course, there's a recession which hasn't helped, people cutting their orders. It chugs along, it just about pays its way.

We toured Frances' nine poly tunnels in the fading November light. On our way out Frances showed me the favourite hiding place for the garden snails in her ecology experiment. There had been about thirty of them and the experiment had something to do with food preferences. Each snail had his own flower pot filled with potting compost and the food he was supposed to eat and a clear plastic pint tumbler placed on top of it all so Frances could observe them. Trouble was, if a snail could get one little toe under his beaker, he would be out and off, travelling great distances in the night. So every morning of her experiment, Frances had to round up the delinquents. They especially liked the space between the counter and the washing machine. For breeding, they preferred the bathroom and Frances said she just lay there in her bath one night watching them do it. And that they were every bit as interesting as the books say.

Growing in peat and quail compost within the tunnels were great expanses of leaves – chervil, parsley, mache, Italian spinach, fancy mustard, and the latest fashion, new pea shoots – Autumn Bliss raspberries, baby dark-red chicory, wild cress, Chinese kale, romaine lettuce, US cress, sorrel, onions, nasturtiums, garlic, chives, Japanese wine berries, yellow September raspberries, English hot black peppermint.

Frances was vibrant, striding up and down on the newspaper-magazine paths. The OU made it all live. She had only to look at the earthworm residue near some sprouting shoots to enthuse about balanced ecosystems involving mineral content, root hairs, pests, acid–alkaline balance, sticky paper with dead insects. The function of sticky paper is to warn Frances when aphids are due. They are treated only with soapy water. The only thing between Park Hill and truly organic farming is the slug pellet, without which there wouldn't be any leaves at all.

I didn't get to see her 2,000 quail because they panic massively at the sight of strange humans. In spite of being hand-raised for 4,000 years and getting along fine with people on an individual quail-to-human basis, flock behaviour takes over when they feel threatened.

But I was assured that these were not battery quail. They run and fly about in spacious aviaries that recreate the dry, warm conditions of North Africa, way out there at the far end of the Marsh Link railway line.

Chapter 10

Early Educational Failure

I loved primary and junior school, but as soon as I went to secondary school I just rebelled and went downhill. I simply hated it and played truant all the time. I just found school really boring. No matter how good you were in some subjects, you were still put down for the things you were bad at. 'You won't amount to anything, Martina Cole,' said the teachers. 'You'll spend all your life just getting by on a laugh.' So I left school at 15 (which was illegal) with no qualifications . . . (Martina Cole, 1993, who received a £150,000 advance on her first novel)

Agonizing over Who'll Make the Grade . . . Teachers Angered by Prospect of Return to O-levels . . . Teachers Unite against Fairy-tale Testing . . . so went the headlines in 1992 as teachers and assessors rebelled against putting selection and segregation back into the education system. How many bad grades must be given along with the good? What percentage of children must fail tests so that standards are maintained? How many students must be losers so that a few can be winners?

'It is our besetting sin, the "English sickness" in education,' wrote Eric Bolton (1992), former senior Chief HM Inspector and professor of education. 'Where we fail badly, in comparison with other developed countries, is with the broad range of ordinary pupils, the middle range and just below, of academic ability. We turn most of those out of our school system under-educated and under-qualified. English education's greatest success throughout its history has been to fail most children. Our system is better than any other in the developed world at failing people, and turning them out with a sense that they have achieved nothing of value.'

What better proof of Professor Bolton's conjecture than a table showing the percentage of 16-year-olds in full-time education and training in various developed countries. There's Canada with 100 per cent, the US with 94 per cent, Japan with 93 per cent and the Netherlands with 93 per cent. Is Spain the lowest with 68 per cent? No. One country is lower – the United Kingdom with 50 per cent (McGiffen, 1993). The UK also has the lowest percentage at age 17 still in school, 35 per cent.

What does the early experience of failure feel like?

Mary Ingham (1981) passed the 11-plus exam and was surprised that *boys* actually failed it. She saw boy and girl failures alike banished to the secondary modern, and she sensed that she, too, was on the verge of failing had she not gone to a girls' school.

> We had our own world, and you could go right to the top of it. With the boys I feel sure we should have shrunk into the old stereotypes, where they forged ahead while we froze into giggling self-consciousness or frittered ourselves away on dog-like devoted attentiveness in class. They would have claimed physics and chemistry, leaving us to potter on with soft-bellied biology, and of course the arts. But [here] the only candidates for the newly refurbished science laboratories were us. (p.52)

Even so, when Ingham later faced the choice of arts versus science courses, like most of her classmates, she chose what she was most successful at. For Ingham – even within the safe confines of English courses – to get marked down made her instantly question her goal of becoming a journalist. She says: 'I was apparently exhibiting a classic female response to failure. Studies of girls' under-achievement argue that girls shrink from challenge, lower their sights earlier than boys because they equate success with luck and failure with lack of ability, whereas boys react the other way round. Boys are better able to combat failure simply because they externalize it. In a way, I did try harder, not so much to prove myself but from sheer terror of failure' (pp. 77–8).

Harassment and domination by boys wear away girls' academic self-esteem, but teachers' attitudes about 'women's proper place' also wear it away. Among a group of science teachers, almost half thought women were not as good as men at 'complicated technical matters', and 42 per cent agreed that 'a woman's career is not as important as a man's'. While only 29 per cent thought a woman's place was in the home, 71 per cent said women should have children only if they were prepared to give up their jobs until the children were in school (Spear, 1985).

How does early educational failure affect mature women?

Studies done by such organizations as Access to Learning for Adults show that the overwhelming majority of women returning to study, at whatever level, left school at the end of their compulsory term with few, if any, qualifications. Unqualified people get labelled by the education system as 'failures' and they carry this stigma throughout their lives. Many women enrolling in access courses do not perceive that the system failed them, and believe that they are not clever enough to enter anything else and do not have the right to become a 'real' student (Sperling, 1989).

Echoing Martina Cole's memories, a common theme among adults studying at an urban polytechnic was the negativism they felt towards their early schooling. Weil (1986) quotes one of a group of 25 white working-class women: 'The teachers were like aliens from another planet. They had different accents, different ways. No idea about working-class behaviours and attitudes. Their lives were so removed from ours. I never regarded school as a learning place' (p. 224). These women did have 'learner identities' but they learned on the street, in their homes, and from life experience.

Marion Jack (1987) knows a lot about Strathclyde women who have got up the nerve to try school again. What are their past images of attending school? Images of 'authoritarian officials, immutable timetables, externally-imposed rules, of rigidly traditional curricula, and of "failure"; the institutionalized flavour of the whole experience had left them with a sense of alienation such that "Education" was not for them. . . .'

'Most of us had had unsatisfactory experiences at school, leaving with few qualifications and a wariness of teachers,' Judy Giles (1990) said of herself as a working-class married mother of three. But after three years of study with the Open University, Judy Giles transferred to York University and in five years had earned a doctorate. In spite of having come so far, she finds it hard to shed her old self-doubt. Her self-image shifts from 'Dr Giles, lecturer' to 'Judy, part-time secretary, housewife and mother'. She sometimes irrationally feels that the academic skills she has gained might be taken away and that working-class folks like her can never be part of the middle-class intellectual community.

In the next chapter you'll meet Misha Hebel. She didn't feel like a failure in school until A-levels. At this point, at 17, the *lack of expectations* she had internalized from her parents, community and school caught up with her. She literally fled the Isle of Sheppey to an administrative job in London for which she had the statutory five O-levels. It has been a long haul from youthful self-doubts on Sheppey to feeling now that 'I could climb Mount Everest, should I wish to.'

Chapter 11

Misha Hebel *From Receptionist to Management Consultant*

I do not come from a deprived background, but from a very ordinary working-class one. I never thought I'd be a management consultant, but that degree enabled me to compete with regular university students. Nobody in my family had been to university. I was expected to leave and go to work in a bank or a shop. There's such a contrast between my expectations when I left school and when I finished my degree, that even now I cannot quite believe where I am and what I'm doing. I'm dead chuffed with myself for being here.

I first interviewed Misha at 6 p.m. on a dark October night in 1991. It was a long, gusty walk to her block of flats from Wandsworth station. So after I shed my winter coat, I joined her while she put the kettle on. Every inch of the walls of that warm, steamy kitchen was covered by colourful pictures of cats. And on the walls of all her other rooms were overflowing bookshelves and dozens of landscapes and portraits.

For Misha's second interview we met at noon in her cramped office in the Met (Metropolitan Police). Here the walls were bare, the furniture bulky and functional, and the colours institutional white, grey and dark green. And here also was an entirely different Misha. In the flat she'd been without make-up, garbed in a pink sweatsuit, red hair askew, spectacles smudged, and with three tabbies twining their tails about her legs. At the Met she was a firmly striding woman wearing a mid-calf navy skirt with white blouse, black tights and polished shoes, hair brushed back and secured with a large black bow. A little make-up brought out all her best facial features.

Misha was born in August 1961 on the Isle of Sheppey in Kent. Her father, now retired, worked in a factory; her mother was an auxiliary nurse. Her father is Polish, her mother English. Misha has one younger brother, a carpenter and joiner.

She went to a local comprehensive and got the statutory five O-levels to get a job – English, maths, geography, history, art and science. Then at 17 she got a job with the Met as a clerical worker, and at 21 she began her OU studies, completing her honours degree in 1990 at age 29. She is single with no children.

What were your reasons for pursuing an OU degree?

I was a low-grade clerical officer who shuffled papers. I did this from age 17 to 21 and I was working shifts, evenings, nights, not 9 to 5. I was feeling a very big gap in my life. I contemplated doing evening classes, but shift work didn't go along with that. Then my mother saw an advert for the OU and sent off for the application. This big package arrived on my doorstep. 'Thank you for showing interest in the Open University. Here are all the papers. Please take time to read them.' Because I thought my mother was interfering, my first instinct was to throw it away. And then I thought about it. And then I read it. And then I had to admit she was right. Just doing my job and coming home, going out occasionally for a drink with friends, wasn't enough. My mother quite often sends off for things for me. Sometimes it's tea-towels, sometimes it's the Open University. So those are the reasons I began the OU in 1983.

But finally I realized that once I got a degree, maybe I could use it. That didn't dawn on me till near the end. Each year I'd been inspired enough to carry on just for the pleasure of it. I also had this little beacon of my thirtieth birthday and I had certain things I wanted to do by that point. And I thought, what can I do with this degree? I want to have a career, rather than just a job, but I don't know where to go.

I did a summer school and had the opportunity to see a careers adviser at Reading University. And this careers lady was marvellous. I wandered in being very vague, saying, 'I need to do something with my life, help me.' And she said, 'What do you think you're good at? What do you like doing? Are there any particular aspects of the degree you've enjoyed?' And I told her.

And she said, 'Well, I think this is the sort of area you could be looking at.' And she gave me books and I read them and thought, This is what I've been working towards. I had chosen courses that would lead me into management consultancy and operational research. And it went on from there. I realized that regular university students virtually all have honours degrees. So it dawned on me that I ought to get honours and I ought to get a good class of honours to able to compete with regular university students. I started going to careers fairs and writing to firms and just generally finding out about it. There was no stopping me. I knew what I wanted. I got an upper second.

What obstacles did you have to overcome, studying through the OU?

I was pushed into doing A-levels. Teachers said I should do it, that I was bright enough, but I failed them, very definitely. All I wanted to do was leave home, which I did, to go and get an admin job. I applied for jobs in newspapers because I didn't want to stay on Sheppey. I got the job in London with the Met and they fortunately arranged hostel accommodation for me. So at 17 I did have somewhere to go.

I wanted to be financially independent. Nobody else in the family had gone to university, so it really didn't cross my mind as a serious possibility. Also, my school wasn't very university-orientated. I can remember people going about with UCCA application forms, but it wasn't pushed. Quite a few students went off to work in banks and building societies, which is all we've got on the Island. I don't know what the teachers thought they were preparing us for.

Then later, when I was studying with the OU, people think you're exceptionally clever, the old brainbox, if you study maths. People don't like brainboxes, and that I found an obstacle. I used to take my studying into work sometimes and work through the lunchbreaks, and if I was seen doing that in the canteen, they'd say, 'Oh, I hated maths in school.' The men I've met through the OU aren't intimidated by apparently clever women, but some police officers are.

But my biggest achievement was overcoming my *own* attitudes and expectations of life. My biggest obstacles were entirely within myself. Although somebody contributed to them, my parents, my school, people I've met, it was mostly all within myself.

And what I have gained, as a woman, is confidence. Confidence that I have the right to be intelligent and the right to do what I want to do. A lot of women don't believe they have the right to deal with their own needs, particularly women with families, either their parents or their own children. Another obstacle – in my early days with the OU I kept quieter than in my later days. Not because the other students were men, but because we were groups and I was afraid of saying something and being wrong. But now I'm not afraid to say anything in any kind of group.

I've learned what you might call tricks. Visualizing myself as being successful, remembering speaking to people in the past when I did well. Getting the OU degree plays a very big part in remembering past successes and knowing I can do what's before me. I visualize the piece of paper that shows the last course I took, the most important one, one I got a distinction for.

What does the OU mean to you?

It means increased self-respect. The Met has had a corporate identity project going for the past couple of years called the Plus Programme. And part of this programme was to have everybody from the organization go along to a one-day seminar to discuss a mission statement. I went along to mine and in the past I probably wouldn't have said anything. Or if I had, I would have blustered and gone red and not been able to come up with any facts. But I was able to put points forward. We were not only talking about the organization, but external influences and politics, subjects I would not have felt comfortable enough to have spoken about before.

Another example is the fact that I believe I can achieve anything I put my mind to. Although my father's Polish, I was never taught Polish as a child, and I recently started to do that. It's very difficult. There are seven cases, a third gender. I am very daunted by it but I will not give up. I've been to Poland a few times, only once in my adult life, but I always had my father to translate, so my knowledge is tiny.

Another of my ambitions is to be a translator. Having goals, having TMAs to go for, having exams, being able to get a credit at the end of it, I need that. So to get a qualification is my first aim, to be able to translate is another, and then to go to Poland and apply the skills I've learned as a management consultant would be quite nice.

I also paint and my confidence with the painting has improved as well. I'm a lot more aware of marketing: I exhibit at crafts fairs and exhibitions. The OU taught me a systematic way of going out and finding what was there, what the market was like, what was happening, what I should do, where I should go. So I have two ambitions. I want to be a famous artist as well as a famous management consultant. The OU's taught me to bite off more than I can chew.

Has the OU changed your life in any other way?

Well, I'm no longer Catholic. I'm thinking of becoming a Quaker. The beliefs behind my becoming a Quaker were there a long time, but I felt I could carry on without attaching myself to a particular denomination. And for a long while the OU was almost my church, it gave me meaning and purpose in life. When that was finished, I think I was looking for something else, and found the Quakers' beliefs were very similar to the ones I held.

It doesn't sound very scientific, but I came across the Wandsworth Meeting House on a bus. I just happened to look out of the window, I saw it there, and I thought, That's where I'm going to be on Sunday. I noticed the time they were having a meeting and on Sunday I got up and I went. The meeting is basically held in silence. And as people are moved to speak, they do. And I sat there in silence reading the little leaflets they had given me. And I felt a very strong feeling of love going around the room. And some people stood up and spoke and what they had to say, it struck a chord.

They have an almost intellectual interest in religion. Not only their own but others, which I wouldn't have found interesting if I hadn't been trained by curiosity at the OU. But the meetings meet my emotional needs as well. For example, I was having problems with my father, we weren't seeing eye to eye. And I was sitting there chatting away to God, asking him, 'Where should I go, what should I do?' Deliberating. And then one of the people stood up and started talking about his own father and their different beliefs, and his own children and how important they were. And he said there was no time for petty squabbles. And there was my answer.

Can you give me some examples of how the OU impacts on your career?
The value of researching and of preparation is something I definitely learned from the OU. Going off and finding books, talking to people. Next week I'm looking at how the typing pool runs at one particular station. But last week on a course on effective presentation skills I met somebody who runs a typing pool somewhere else. She had very clear ideas of how it ran and the problems. So I'm going to see her next week before I go off and see the other people, and read any literature we have on how typing pools run.

Never miss an opportunity, that's from the OU as well. That there's a great value in opportunities and you shouldn't miss something just because you don't feel quite up to it. It's very easy to say, 'Oh, yeah, I'll do that,' and then put it off. Whereas if you actually grasp it, take it, and keep at it, then it's worth it in the long run. I could easily have given up, a couple of times, with the OU, and not sent in assignments. But the benefit I gained from sending in every assignment, not skipping any, was so valuable, it helped me so much when it came to the exam.

I had an interview for promotion last year and got it. My preparation beforehand was thorough. I spoke to people. I read books. I talked to people in the organization, outside the organization, who'd been to promotion boards. People who sat on promotion boards who were friends of mine. My preparation was unbelievably thorough and very time-consuming.

Also, I try not to make face-value judgements. In conjunction with one of the last courses I did, T301 Systems Thinking, systems thinking is all about thinking about situations as a whole, not just looking at numbers and facts and figures. You have to look at the interplay between people and how they react and the little hierarchies and empires people build, and the way some people don't like talking to other people, and how some people don't like using computers. If there's a certain kind of behaviour, there'll be reasons behind it. For example, when I used to work as a receptionist at the police station, you get people coming in who are mentally ill. And they like to pay visits to the police.

What I discovered, partly because of the OU, was that there was a cause for every single behaviour and usually all these people wanted was for you to listen to them. They just want some attention. Before the OU, I wouldn't have wanted anything to do with them at all. But I became quite good, especially with elderly or distressed people.

We used to have one particular gentleman who came in. I would get a call saying, 'There's somebody here to see you,' and I knew exactly who it was because they found him very distressing. He'd been in a concentration camp during the war and he'd got Parkinson's and he thought he was being persecuted.

I must have been about four years into the OU before I applied for that job of station reception officer. I didn't have the confidence to go before. I wouldn't talk to anyone, I was so painfully shy. It looked pretty daunting and I knew I was going to have to face people and I knew there was a lot I was going to have to learn but I wanted to do something more challenging. Then, if I hadn't had the OU, when I stopped being a station reception officer, I would have gone back to being a clerical officer, shuffling papers in an office again.

What is the most important use you make of your OU degree?
The ability to plan and the ability to see a whole situation. Also I've learned a number of techniques to help me to be patient, stand back, look at the situation, don't rush in, don't open your big mouth.

I started with Living with Technology. I had no idea how long and how much planning it took to implement major technologies. It's very interesting now to look back because the things that the course was predicting then are commonplace now, like the supermarkets with their screens and barcoding. That was virtually theory and experimental at that point.

I have what is called in the real world an operational research degree. The OU doesn't call it that. It had a very common theme about looking at the world and problems and ways of solving them. I'm a 'management scientist' with the Met police. Behind the visible face of police work, the detectives and the constables, there is a whole lot of back-up. There are people processing parking tickets. There are people in administration offices at police stations who have to work out transfers and overtime pay. The support services are quite immense and very often ignored in popular television shows. Because it's such a large organization with a great many different types of staff, they have problems. And we get called in to solve those problems.

The Met needs a huge personnel database, needs to keep track of who's where and who has done what. It's all been paper records up until recently. There is also a crime computer called CRIS. I work on the fringes of that. I also solve very standard management consultancy problems. It can be very small-scale, doing number crunching working out how many forms somebody should order in a week. Or maybe stores has a huge pile of form 900s and nobody's ordering them, so we have to find out why.

How did you balance your OU studies with work and the rest of life?
It wasn't too difficult because I've been single throughout and I've worked shifts, which meant that a lot of the time I had free was other people's working hours. So if I shared a flat with someone, it was quiet. Work I couldn't change so I had to go around that. With

people I'd weigh up the pros and cons and if I had a TMA, I'd stay in and do it. Of course, I enjoyed it, I wasn't just doing them to gain an academic achievement.

The boyfriend I had when I first started with the OU thought it was ridiculous that I was doing it, particularly because I had chosen technology. He probably would have coped better if I had chosen arts or sociology. But technology – 'Why do you want to do that? Why would a woman want to do that?' He didn't last very long.

What was the hardest part of OU study? The easiest part?

The hardest was sitting down and preparing a TMA, gathering my thoughts, particularly as the deadline got nearer. I'm a bit of a last-minute person. I suppose the easiest was the summer school because you have lots of support there. You might actually do stuff that is academically difficult, but you're not the only one. And the majority of people would go along to summer school feeling they were fed up, they wanted to pack it in, and by the end of it, people would say, 'Well, I'm going to finish this. This is great.' They'd made new contacts to help them carry on or they had just gained confidence.

I picked my courses so they'd have summer schools, so I've done five and one weekend school. They were all good. Most memorable was TM282 Modelling with Mathematics. It was the one where I came away thinking I learned the most. But the male–female ratio was very distorted. There was about one woman to every 20 men and they had us with another course, again very male-dominated, and I don't think we managed more than a dozen women between the two. The OU had its traditional disco despite this male–female ratio and the idiocy of the arrangement brought people together, so we spent the time in the bar talking, with the music going on in the background.

What are the advantages of an OU degree and the disadvantages?

One is timing, being able to fit it around your lifestyle. But another advantage is being able to grow and develop with it. The system whereby you only choose a year ahead at a time means you can switch directions. I did switch directions at one point, which I wouldn't have done if I hadn't gone to summer school and chatted with Clifford, this guy from Northern Ireland, about the social science course. I was going to go for all the hard stuff, but he impressed me so much that I did the social sciences foundation and economics and politics, subjects that I hadn't touched and knew nothing about. I got a taste for them and I shifted over to a more people-orientated approach.

As for disadvantages, with hindsight and now wanting to take my career a lot further, I would have preferred to have gone to a regular university. An OU degree is always acknowledged as being good, but it's acknowledged as being good for different reasons. A regular university is considered to be good because, especially if it's Oxford or Cambridge, it's the academic standard that is acknowledged. With the OU, it is the inconvenience and the determination and the fact that you've given up your own time and money to work at the degree. The OU showed what I'm best at, which is a terrier-like persistence, but I also feel I'm on a par with any graduate.

What was your success with the OU due to?

Like I've said, dogged persistence. I was not going to fail. 'I will not be beaten' is a phrase I come out with occasionally. My partner and I are contemplating buying a house together. It's fraught with difficulties as my parents don't like him and financially it could have difficulties. At one point we discovered that maybe we couldn't get the mortgage we wanted. And he said 'Oh, well, it was a good idea but it was just a dream.' Well, I will not be beaten. And the look in my eye. We left the conversation there and a couple of days later, he said, 'You were quite right. Let's stick at it.' And we've sorted out most of the problems.

What was most important in your life before the OU, and after?

Before? Men. Boys. Relationships, that was it, I wasn't doing anything else. I only had one shelf of books. Going to work, coming home, going out in the evening. Mostly down to the pub, the occasional trip to the cinema.

At the moment it's my partner, but he is more or less equal to my job and my painting, they're all equal. My job is very important because it is the proof of my OU degree. The better I can do the job, the better my OU degree speaks for itself. If I do badly, there are plenty who are going to turn around and say, 'She's the first OU graduate that we've ever taken and the academic standard is obviously not good.' So I want to prove to the people I work for that I'm as good as any regular graduate.

Would you have been interested in your partner before the Open University?

Possibly not. No. He's got a mind full of trivia and interesting information. He's very quick, very sharp and quite competitive. In the past he would have been too much for me. In a very friendly way we try to score points the whole time, but job-wise and academically, we don't compete.

I met him through the job. He intrigues me. He's a policeman. He has virtually no education. He left school very young and went into the army as a cadet. He was in the army 8 or 9 years, had some manual and industrial jobs and joined the police eight years ago. He's a constable who walks a beat, at the moment. He really likes helping people.

What are your career plans?

Now that I know I can do my job, and I know I could go on further, I'm happy with that. It's almost as if I've proved the point I wanted to make. Job-wise, academically, I've proved myself. So part of me wants to go off and do things I really love doing. Which is painting. I'm trying to find a compromise. I don't have enough control over what I'm doing at work. I'm a very small cog in a big wheel and I'd like to be a bigger cog in a smaller wheel. I've been with the department ten years now. And with the Met, twelve. That's a big part of who I am, who I've become, my job.

Of all the friends Misha made at summer school, Clifford is remembered the most fondly and after ten years, they still write on a regular basis. Because of her social science courses, Misha said, she came to understand why he stays in Northern Ireland – he wants to teach there, his family is there, his heritage is there. Is Clifford the inspiration for Misha's hankering to be a famous artist and a famous management consultant – in Poland?

Chapter 12

Low Self-Confidence

What happens in a school where you've got good sporty people is that the whole school becomes sportified. If you were a girl and you wanted to play football, you could. . . . So I took up just about everything, pentathlon (high jump, long jump, hurdles, shot put and 200 metres) and I played county hockey, county netball and tennis for the school. I think competitiveness is a must in life. Not your first priority, but everybody, sometime, somewhere, is going to come up against barriers he or she has got to be aggressive to get through. The good thing about Barbara Richards was that she kept telling me I could be the best out there. Even if you don't believe it yourself at the time, if someone keeps telling you, you grow to believe it and probably it helps to bring out whatever it is that is there. (Tessa Sanderson, MBE, winner of Commonwealth and Olympic gold medals, interviewed by Susan Thomas, 1992)

When girls' self-confidence in school actually rises, it doesn't just happen. It requires some giant gesture such as the Assertiveness Training Programme started at Stoke Newington School in 1980. An anti-sexist group established girls-only space inside and outside the school building, single-sex counselling and tutorial times, single-sex groups or individual support for maths, physics and chemistry, and various spurs to get pupils thinking about non-traditional courses and jobs. But what did the most for the girls' self-confidence was single-sex assertiveness training (Cornbleet and Libovitch, 1983).

What happens in schools to undermine girls' and teenagers' self-confidence?

Nursery schools do girls a big disservice when they do nothing to encourage play with toys non-traditional for one's sex. Boys are automatically given construction games such as Lego and Meccano by their parents. This kind of play gives them practice at manipulating objects, and spatial and mechanical skills give boys feelings of self-confidence and self-control over the world. Primary schools could provide girls with the same construction toys, says Jane French (1990), to make up for what girls are not getting at home and bring them up to par with boys. Then, it is fervently hoped, girls later would not reject school subjects which require manipulating objects, such as physics.

After nursery school's *non-intervention* in traditional girls' play, comes instruction in reading, writing and arithmetic. Girls' memories go something like this: 'At school they all used to laugh at you.' 'Yes they did and I think that stuck in a lot of ways.' 'You were frightened of putting your hand up in case you were wrong, but not now.' (Returners' conversation, quoted in Hughes and Kennedy, 1985, p. 170).

To combat classroom jeering and ridicule, the headteacher of South Hampstead High School – after looking at the extensive research on the impact of boys on girls in co-ed schools – comes out solidly in favour of single-sex girls' schools. When sexual harassment is *not* a part of daily life, as it is *not* in girls' schools, girls have higher self-esteem, greater self-confidence, better examination passes (particularly in the sciences and mathematics), more genuine subject choice (more girls choose maths, physics and chemistry at advanced levels), and, last, more chances to be leaders (Burgess, 1990).

I found that Her Majesty's Inspectorate agrees with Burgess' conclusion (Department for Education, 1992). HMI's survey of eight schools in two local education authorities found self-confidence and aspiration higher among girls in girls-only schools than in mixed schools.

The inspectors found that mixed schools, by contrast, did *not* challenge girls' traditional choices and did little to raise girls' expectations. For example:

> In some lessons boys were encouraged to express ideas more fully than girls. Occasionally, girls under-valued themselves, under-achieved and even allowed boys or male teachers to do work for them. One group of girls, for example, avoided solving mathematical problems by resorting to the boys for help; then they demanded attention from the male teacher who provided answers rather than challenging them to think for themselves. In the girls' schools with a predominance of female staff, dependent behaviour of this type was not possible. (p. 7)

Girls at girls' schools said these schools gave them confidence by pushing them and not allowing them to fail; they were encouraged to ask questions; they were encouraged to plan ahead; they were not put down for their weaknesses.

How does lack of academic self-confidence affect us as adult learners?

Even young women of high ability watch their self-confidence erode away in a mixed-sex setting. Kim Thomas's *Gender and Subject in Higher Education* (1990) is devoted to 48 women and 48 men studying either physics or English at three universities. One of her conclusions was

> how much more self-confident the men were than the women. This was particularly striking amongst the female physics students, especially those who had been to single-sex schools: they were bright, intelligent and able, yet they felt unsure of themselves in the environment of a university physics department. These were women whose self-image was undergoing a change: in school, they were clever, confident students who would have successful careers as physicists. University challenged that identity. (p. 181)

Because of low self-confidence, countless mature women choose to return to school in the relaxed environment of further education classes. Then, their confidence boosted, they go on to do degrees, reports Joan Davies, vice-chairman of the National Federation of Women's Institutes (1991). Women, more than men, she says, suffer from low academic self-confidence, especially after being at home with children. How discriminatory and counter-productive it would be for the government to cut back funding of informal, non-vocational classes in favour of classes directly linked to jobs.

Women's intelligence has sometimes also been put down by the men in their families. Margaret MacIntosh (1990), who has taught in community schools for years, told the story of a young woman who returned to do just one O-level. She got her certificate for the sole purpose of throwing it down in front of her father and brothers and saying, 'There, you see?' Not surprisingly, 'An increase in self-confidence is an observable result for those women who come back and finish a course. It does not matter much whether the class is a vocational one or a recreational one' (p. 61).

Ann Wickham (1986) agrees with MacIntosh. She says that courses such as 'New Opportunities for Women' or 'Fresh Horizons' are essentially counselling to increase self-confidence so that women can return to work. The courses' success lies in reassuring students that other women have the same self-doubts. Sometimes the rise in morale is such that women go on to higher education rather than a job.

Kushalta Saini, who tells her story in the next chapter, had one year of a girls-only secondary school, but then the school changed into a comprehensive, a mixture of boys and girls. Kush went from outgoing and friendly to very shy and withdrawn. It wasn't until she was 16 that she started to get her confidence back. Kush passed seven O-levels, but failed to get the two A-levels necessary for university, a setback to her academic confidence. But the combination of succeeding simultaneously at the OU *and* at work has given her confidence enough to succeed also as a performing artist.

What did I say at the beginning of this essay? When women's self-confidence in school actually improves, it doesn't just happen? Because not any and every effort at further education increases women's self-confidence. In 1991 Jean Kelly studied the speech of women and men doing a training course for supervisors at a community school in Hounslow. Quite simply, she recorded the minutes each person spoke and the number of turns each person took speaking. The men dominated the talk on both scores. But that wasn't all. While the women were co-operative in their speech, the men ignored what the women said and took over discussions to make their points by using coarse language and insults. In the end, they silenced the women.

You'll be glad to know that OU tutors are trained *not* to let this happen in tutorials, but after their first foundation course, OU women can hold their own, just fine.

Chapter 13

Kushalta Saini *From Clerical Officer to Executive 3 Clerk*

I do want to settle down, my father's gone, and if something happened to my mother, I'm virtually on my own. But I won't just blindly go into marriage. I'll be very careful and I'll hang on to the things that matter to me. Also I have gone through difficulties in life to get to this level and I'm not going to let go of that security.

The first time I met Kush was in her home, so I didn't notice how diminutive she is. The second time I met her, in the doorway of the Dominion Theatre on Tottenham Court Road, suddenly she was there in front of me, smiling up. I had been intently scanning faces from 5 foot 7 inches. To spot Kush's face in the crowd you have to look *way* down. She is petite, brown-skinned, has beautiful dark eyes and hair, and likes to wear black with a sparkle of silver jewellery and a diamond in her nose.

Kush was born in 1961 in London. Her parents came here from North India in 1957. Her father was an architect, and her mother has worked her way up from copy typist to senior administrative officer for the UKCC for Nursing, Midwifery & Health Visitors. Kush went to a local primary school, a mixed comprehensive, and retook her A-levels at a private school in Kensington. She passed seven O-levels, including English, Latin, maths and French, and one A-level in English. Her OU studies began in 1983; she concentrated on the social sciences and got her degree in 1990 when she was 28. Her father was on a kidney machine for 26 years and died in 1987. Like her mother, Kush has worked her way up in administration, starting with ILEA and functioning currently as the clerk to the Civil Defence Committee for the London Fire and Civil Defence Authority.

Kush can speak and write Hindi but doesn't consider herself fluent because in speaking she mixes Hindi with Punjabi and English. She learned Punjabi at home, but not because it was demanded of her, as was true for many of her friends. I got the feeling that her mother liked speaking Punjabi at home, just as she preferred a sari to Western clothes.

What were your reasons for doing an OU degree?

I started my job when I was 18 and the idea was that I would leave eventually and go to university. But I had a boss who gave me encouragement and I gained a lot of confidence in what I was doing. And before I knew it, they told me to apply for promotion. Then it came to me, I don't really want to leave, because I feel like I'm getting somewhere.

Suddenly I thought, Hang on a minute, I'll combine the two things, the studying and the working, because I was very determined I wanted a degree, and I wanted to do it in subjects that I chose. I wanted flexibility. My mother had taken social science with the OU and my Dad gave her encouragement.

So I told my father and he was thrilled and he saw the way I was getting on at work and he said, 'I've made the greatest mistake as a father because I've tried to push you into my profession and your talents lie in writing.' And he said, 'I'm really glad you want to further your studies and you do whatever you want to do.' So I got all the prospectuses, and in those days you couldn't start until 22, so I had to wait.

Did you have any other obstacles besides your father's illness to overcome?

To be honest, I can't remember when he was well. I remember waking up in the middle of the night and finding nobody in the house because my father had to be rushed off to be declotted and my mother had to do that at 3 o'clock in the morning when you haven't got time to sort things out, and Mum said often she'd find me sitting on the steps, waiting for them to come back from the hospital.

I was very much a loner, shy and insecure. Maybe if I'd had brothers and sisters, it might have been different. But it was my mum, my dad, myself. I felt I had to give my friends presents in order to make friendships. And I had some beautiful things at home, sent to me from India, and I would find myself giving them away in order to get friendship. And if I had a hard teacher, I used to get tearful. Once I had a very strict teacher and we had handwriting tests and I wanted to be meticulous but an individual as well, and I thought the very best handwriting would be to separate all the letters out. I thought I'd done a wonderful job but my teacher put me in detention because she thought it was awful. It was somebody's birthday and she said, 'You won't get a piece of cake for it because you've done so badly.'

Moving on to secondary school, a girls' school for a year, that first year was fine. Then that school became a comprehensive, a mixture of boys and girls. I didn't know how to cope, and I became very shy and withdrawn again. And it wasn't until I was 16 or 17 that I started getting my confidence back.

Years later, when I was upstairs doing an OU essay, my father would say, 'You don't spend any time with me.' And I'd say, 'On the one hand you're happy that I'm doing a degree, but on the other hand you don't want me studying.' But during those final two years he could see I was on my own feet. He'd say, 'She's my son and she's my daughter. I only want the best.' And when people would come to our house, it was embarrassing because he'd talk about me, 'She got such and such grade at the OU.' He was so proud.

What sorts of impacts did your OU studies have on your career?

What happened in my job at ILEA was great. What I gained a lot personally from the OU was discipline. After a year I applied for promotion to Executive 1 and I got it, and I was only in that job for six months and they moved me to another section which was even more demanding. I was managing teaching centres, which really did stretch me. And then I applied for Executive 2 and I didn't get it, but they liked me at the interview because I was able to relate how I studied at the OU to the job, where it was important to read through material very quickly to grasp the main points and write something. I said in the interview that I had to do that anyway with the Open University, and that worked in my favour.

They liked me so much they seconded me to work on a political front, the Save ILEA

Campaign. I was then working closely with very senior officers and members of the Authority and members of Parliament, helping to prepare briefs. I got to work with good officers, and my boss was doing a PhD at the time and she was very encouraging with my OU. I'm going to backtrack just for a second, to when I was working at teachers' centres, that boss was also doing Open University, and he gave me his essays to glance through. He was constantly encouraging me, and if I had to do an urgent assignment, he understood. We had libraries at work, so I could go there, so I had it all.

After the Save ILEA Campaign I took an Executive 2 acting position where I worked closely with schools, seeing the other end of the education system, basically. Again a very demanding job but with people who appreciated that I was studying as well. After that I was asked to apply for other jobs at that grade. I was unsuccessful twice and then on the third attempt I got an Executive 2 in the committee secretariat at headquarters. And I moved back there and spent two and a half years. This boss had just started the OU so that was great, I had someone else. By this time I knew of so many people doing the OU, it was quite incredible.

I spent two years there and then ILEA was going and this job came up with the London Fire and Civil Defence Authority at the Executive 3 level. And I thought, It's not an area I would love to go into, but why not? And out of 60 to 70 applications, I was shortlisted, had the interview and got the job.

I'm in the Committee Secretariat. I'm clerk to the Civil Defence Committee; all civil defence issues are taken by that committee and it is attended by local councillors. Apart from arranging the meetings and the usual things, I advise them procedurally at meetings, how they are to go about business. I get reports from professional officers who are often ex-army people, and I have to read and understand these reports fully and if that committee forwards a report to a higher committee, it is my responsibility to do the report. I've done this since March 1989.

Did the OU affect in any way your ideas about success?

My idea of success is having your aim on something and working hard for it. I had a hard struggle academically in terms of O-levels and A-levels and I watched all my friends get their success and go straight into university and I'm working so hard but nothing is coming along. Is there something wrong? Am I not capable? I had very low self-esteem, but I said to myself, Don't give up, it'll come your way. Instead of getting from A to B in a very direct way of O-levels, A-levels, degree, I went O-levels, take them again, have a hard time with A-levels, start working, get a little bit of experience there, and then do it the hard way of studying and working together to get my degree.

What is the most important use you make of your OU degree?

Recognizing people in the office who have a burning desire to do something like the OU but feel they're incapable and being able to say, 'I know what you're going through. Can I do it? Am I good enough?' I had a very hard home life but I didn't have a family and children. Especially the women in my office who have got those commitments find it very difficult to break out. I have started a women's support group. It happened because I went on a Women and Management course with another colleague. We did a lot of assertiveness training and career planning. We discussed common problems in the organization we're in, where we deal with a lot of uniformed staff, ex-army people who find it very difficult working with women. Equal opportunities policies are way beyond them.

After this course the head clerk, a very astute woman, called the two of us in and said, 'There's an initiative to start a women's support group. It's under my remit but I want the two of you to set it up.' The proposal only came to us in April of this year but since then we've managed to get the steering group together and to get women to come to the sessions. There are two sides to the women's support group. One is training and career development, the other is a network of support for women who want to talk to one another.

One of my colleagues feels she hasn't got a direction in life now, and she feels she needs to do some sort of studying, so I said, 'How about the OU? And if you don't want to do a degree, you can do an associate course, a short course.' So she's thinking about it. Another of my friends has just been made redundant and she left school with nothing. And she feels, 'It's impossible, it's been so many years since I've done anything.' And I said, 'Well, the OU also runs returning to study courses.' Because I got something out of it, I am able to give them enthusiasm, as opposed to, 'Oh, God, it's such a drag.'

At work the other day, in some meeting, everybody acknowledged how few women there were in the higher grades, full stop. I looked around and thought, I'm the only Asian in my grade in this room, the only person with two Asian parents. So my heart goes out to women who are the only woman in an office full of men.

Can you give me an example of a transfer from your liberal arts studies to your job?
I do a lot of writing in my job. That experience of seven years of writing essays for the OU gave me confidence in writing reports. This February in my grade we were on six months of seconding within the section just to get a feel for another person's job. I did exactly what I was doing there but for the Fire Brigade. The head of the clerks to the authority is a perfectionist, very demanding. She knew when I was doing the Open University, and although she's incredibly busy, she always took time to find out, 'How's it going? Have you done it?' She knew when I'd passed it and was very happy.

Anyway, I was in this new job and I had to clerk a very difficult meeting to do with a complaint from a member of Parliament. And suddenly a report that takes eight weeks to do had to be done in ten working days. She called me up to her office and said, 'I know you know nothing about the subject but this is going to be your development task. You've got to extract information, you've got to do the framework of the report, you got to do this, this, this.' It was pretty terrifying. But she looked at me and she said, 'You've done the OU, so I'm sure you had to do things like this and I want you to apply it now.' It had been a year since I did the OU, and I thought, How do I do it? I basically ate, drank and slept that report. After I did the framework, she challenged me on every point. 'There's always this and there's always that.' And I could feel the OU coming back to me, that all-sides approach, the balanced argument. So I went away and I applied what I'd done at the OU about your beginning, your middle and your conclusion, your recommendations, and I extracted information from different departments just as I would extract information for the OU. And in the end I got there from the confidence of knowing I was able to write.

How was the OU right for you?

I had the best of every world by doing the OU. I wanted to work, I wanted to get higher in my grade, I wanted to further my career, I wanted to have a degree, and I didn't want to be bound by going to this tutorial, that tutorial. Another big thing was it wasn't too exam-orientated. It took into consideration the work you did outside those three exam hours. I liked that mixture, which you don't get with A-levels and O-levels. I did a hell of a lot of work for my O-levels, but my father, unfortunately, was taken very ill when I was doing them and, of course, I flunked them the first time. My father wrote to the examination board and said, 'I was given the wrong drugs and actually turned blind for nine months, putting increasing pressure on my family.' But there was only a little weight that could be given to that.

Whereas at the OU I could say, 'These are my circumstances, I'll try and keep up as best I can.' The greatest thing was during my last year when my father passed away. That year I was getting extremely high grades on my assignments, 95s, 98s, and I thought I can try for a distinction this year in my exams. But my father died and I had to phone up and ask to be exempted from one of the assignments. And they said, 'You've got the grades so don't worry about it.' I had in fact to leave two assignments and I went in cold to do my exam. But I kept my average and that was very important.

I was financed the first year with the OU through my borough, Brent. And the next year I got half, then a quarter, then nil. And the people at work asked why I didn't try for financing through work. But I didn't want to associate it with work because I knew the organization would be on my back: 'Have you passed? Have you done this? Have you done that?' I didn't want it to be like the life-and-death struggle when you're doing O-levels and A-levels – if you didn't get it, then what? I wanted to do it in my own time. I could stop it for a year if need be, or take a half credit, and that would do me fine.

What were the easiest and hardest parts of studying with the OU?

Although it seemed hard at first, I've loved every summer school. The social science foundation was in Sussex. I was 22 and I met lots and lots of people in their thirties. They all had so much experience and working life that I felt like a little school kid and when we had group discussions, I felt, Oh, my goodness, I don't want to speak, they all know so much more than me. But by the end of the week, I realized that I had a voice and I could participate and join in. And that set me up for the next year when I did Introduction to Psychology, where you couldn't keep me quiet.

I got so much out of the social science summer school that I didn't have to revise for my exam. Because it was all condensed in that week – the major points for each discipline you were studying. They spent a lot of time on the exam. It was basically an intensive revision course. Summer school did it for you, being in that environment, being able to discuss it 24 hours a day, not being distracted. And keeping in touch with those people is great.

At my first summer school I met Caroline, who was a nursery nurse, and we've corresponded ever since. Caroline is now married and has three children and has stopped and started, stopped and started OU. But what we had in common was being young, 22, and from the same part of town. So we stuck together and at my second summer school, arts, I met Pat in the queue waiting for the mini-bus to campus and we realized we were on the same course and became the nucleus for a group which remained solid for a year after we got back.

If you had to do it over again, would you get your degree through the OU?
I've had a lot of people at work say, 'How can you do this for six years? Why don't you just go to university?' They would try and make me see the negative side of it. But my philosophy was if I looked at it as a year at a time, and I'm doing it for my enjoyment, and I'm only choosing the subjects that I like, and I'm not comparing it to what I do at work, then there's more chance of me getting through it.

Today if I was as undecided as I was when I did my A-levels, I'd do the same thing again. But if I was very single-minded and knew exactly what subjects I wanted to do, I'd go to university and do it in three years. At the age of 31 if I wasn't working and I had the chance to study and I was very ready to go university, I'd do it. But in my circumstances at the age of 18 and being so undecided in my life, I would have flunked university if I'd gone.

And through those years of going up in my job, I now feel I haven't missed anything by not going to university when I did. I'm exactly at the same point on the ladder that I would have been if I'd done it the other way.

What quality do you think was most responsible for your success with the OU?
Discipline. I packed more into my life in those seven years than I've ever done. Because now, when you're not doing the OU, you do lots of nothingness. People said, 'You won't have a social life. It's work, work, work, and it's study, study, study.' But I used to tell my friends, 'Well, this weekend I can't go out because I've got a TMA, but next weekend, I'm free.' I never could study during the week in the evenings, I found I was coming home too late. So I did a lot of reading on the train going to work and on the lunch hour, and the bulk of my work was on Sunday. Or I'd take my annual leave and use it for that.

I was able to manage my time very, very well with the OU and organize myself generally. And I accepted that it's not a perfect world; you can't do everything. The first year I started, it was, Oh, I haven't listened to this radio programme, this is really bad. You let things get on top of you. But I learned that one year you might be able to do 95 per cent of the work, but you can't do that every year because there are other things going on in your life. It made me learn how to pick and choose and prioritize what are the important things to do.

What are your career plans over the next five years?
Within the London Fire and Civil Defence Authority I've got a very demanding job and new things are being given to me and that is keeping me motivated. But to be honest, civil defence is not an issue that greatly enthrals me. I have another interest in my life. For fourteen years I've done Indian dancing. I'm a classical dancer and we do a lot of performances and I go regularly to class. There was a time when I went three times weekly to my class but with the OU, home and work, I had to let one of the classes go. I also teach little kids and do lecture demonstrations.

I'd love to do what I'm doing now, committee work, but in an arts environment. At the moment there are lots of cuts and it's not the right time, but I'd love to get into the arts combined with my other skills.

What was most important in your life before the OU and now?

What was most important before the OU was to have that degree, it was this big thing of not letting the family down. Now I just want to be happy in whatever I do.

My job is important. I've still got areas within it to tackle before I can say, I do a good job. I'm not doing it yet the way my expectations of myself say I should. Until I have perfected it, I won't kid myself that I'm ready to go up. I don't have the self-esteem to go up at this stage. There are two more grades and then I become a senior officer. And that's when you're managing a department with twenty or thirty. But the more I'm getting up, the more time it takes to assimilate it.

Last week, for example, I went to a meeting where two political sides were debating and you know there's going to be an amendment and the hardest thing is to say exactly what they mean. I knew an amendment was coming up but it was so complex financially and legally that I could not string my words together. And my boss's boss, that's what she's there for, to help out with those amendments, she said, 'See what they think of these words.' And it got accepted and after the meeting I said to her, 'How do you do it? I wish I could do that.' And even though that is her job, I feel that I should be able to do it. So there are areas where I am lacking, that might not be outwardly apparent to my colleagues, I can improve upon.

In the next five years, I'm single at the moment, I think I'd like to settle down and have a family. The OU has given me my independence. It's allowed me to be myself, but I'm also bound by Indian culture where you must finish your degree and then get married and have a family. But I'm not going to be bound by the arranged way. I'm a bit of a rebel. In my past relationships, especially while the OU was going on, I wouldn't let anything get in the way of it. I'd meet somebody but if he'd say, especially one from India, that marriage was on the cards, my first thought was, I've got to finish my OU first. I can't do anything without that.

Now that I've finished it, seven years is quite enough of the OU. I'm making up for those years, going out and enjoying myself, meeting the people I want to meet with a view to settling down, getting married.

I asked Kush what she thought Indian culture added to traditional English culture and she said, immediately, the warmth of Indian life, the affection, the togetherness. Indians not only value the extended family, but in India, people drop in on one another casually for a cup of tea and a little chat. No one would dream of phoning ahead. That would be considered very cold.

I found out about this warmth at first hand. I was hesitant about sitting in on Kush's dance class. Would they feel I was intruding, invading their private space? But as I entered the room, the teacher, Sunita Golvala, patted a chair beside her for me to sit down. Everyone bowed to her and smiled at me. The music began.

Chapter 14

Male Bias

What can mixed schools do . . . to attract more female pupils by becoming 'girl-friendly'? . . . Not all the girls I spoke to want to do mixed PE and games, but most want the opportunity to play the same games, particularly football and rugby. . . . Another frequent complaint is about the playground being dominated by boys and that there is nowhere for girls to go at break and lunch times. . . . not uncommonly, I am told stories about 'no-go' areas in schools where boys congregate inappropriately to call names or even to touch female pupils passing by. I am still shocked when I hear black girls talk about name-calling and how many of them just resign themselves to it. (Myers, 1992)

Schools' lesser interest in girls doesn't end there. 'Praise bias for boys in school' read a *Guardian* headline (Meikle, 1992). Secondary school boys apparently get more attention from their teachers than do girls. Boys get both more praise from male teachers for good academic work and more reprimands from women teachers for bad behaviour.

Then there is a study that has found 'teachers in mixed schools paid insufficient attention to the ways in which boys sometimes dominate work in classrooms and other key areas of school life'. When boys and girls go to school together, as reported in a survey of schools in Bromley and Nottinghamshire, boys dominate lessons and take charge of activities to the detriment of girls (Department for Education, 1992).

'Both [of our] girls schools have a genuine problem,' said a headteacher, referring to Dartford's Girls Grammar and LEA high school. The problem? The Boys Grammar School, when it opted out of local authority control, took over the sports area which all the schools (two grammars, two secondary modern mixed schools) had shared for decades and put a 2-metre-high spiked metal fence around it (Buckley, 1992). When I showed this article to an American educator, she said, 'Well, the boys themselves surely didn't put up this fence.' Right, I assured her, adult authorities put up the fence; it's a great example of how the system is male-biased.

Boys may be domineering in secondary schools, but does male bias also exist in primary schools?

Yes, it does. Nursery teachers offer far more help to girls than boys, at the same time giving boys more facts and information than girls. And when it comes to play, primary teachers have a look-the-other-way philosophy. Their permissiveness – let the children do what they want and don't intervene – means boys avoid girls' toys and play, and girls learn no boys' games nor how to manipulate boys' toys. Why? Because children act out what they have learned at home is appropriate for girls and for boys. *Unless* teachers encourage cross-sex play – girls playing boys' games and with boys' toys and vice versa – it doesn't happen. This means girls leave school having learned few skills associated with traditionally male activities (French, 1990).

The survey conclusion reported above, that a few boys dominate classes, is shared by French, who reviewed many, many studies all of which pointed to the same conclusion – teachers pay more attention to boys. By the age of 11, French says, girls are a passive audience for certain male 'characters' who are the centre of everyone's attention in class. Worse, what's the educational value, she asks, of teachers making the sexes compete with one another and setting one sex up as a negative reference point? Invariably, it is the girls who are the losers in this competition, for example, when teachers let boys ridicule other boys by calling them 'a load of girls'.

And exactly what happens in secondary school?

'Research conducted in secondary school classrooms has suggested that, as in primary classrooms, boys tend to have the lion's share of teachers' attention,' says French. She illustrates this point by sharing her observations of a mixed-sex, first-year physics class in a school in a prosperous catchment area with good teacher–pupil–parent relationships. It was boys who answered the teacher's questions. It was boys who drew the diagrams on the blackboard. It was boys who performed the demonstration experiments. What did the girls do? They watched.

There was no evidence of sexually explicit harassment in this genteel, middle-class classroom, French said. But malicious sexual harassment is, in fact, the principal way secondary schools are male-biased. One article I cannot get out of my mind was written by Leila (the student) and Susan (the mother) Suleiman in 1985. Leila went to a large comprehensive attended by the borough's lowest ability students. Here the teachers did nothing to stop boys from making school a nightmare for the girls. Teachers allowed boys to taunt, intimidate, even punch and kick girls. What do you think of the Suleimans' explanation? It is not sex-linked but class-linked: 'Schools of this type do not aim to educate children. Instead, they effectively reduce their aspirations, so that they will accept their station in life, and not compete with middle-class children for professional jobs.'

Boys do better in mixed-sex schools than single-sex schools; girls do better in single-sex schools than in mixed-sex schools. The reasons? For the girls is it solely the lack of sexual harassment? Or sexual distraction? Or does it also have to do with expectations? In fact, they are far higher for girls in girls-only schools. For example, Dr Joan Hanafin's recent study in Ireland found co-education had a negative effect on girls' examination performance but not on boys'. Girls in single-sex schools spent more time doing homework, less time doing housework, and were more likely to want and to expect to continue their formal education after they had left school (Walshe, 1992).

But social class still plays a role. Girls' expectations and goals are very different depending on the social class of the single-sex school. For example, Angela Holdsworth (1988) looked at the goals of working-class girls at Parklands Comprehensive in Lancashire, and the goals of middle-class girls at Cheltenham Ladies' College. Parklands' girls want jobs exactly like their mothers, jobs suited to family life – nursery nursing, cooking, teaching, looking after the old. In contrast, 85 per cent of Cheltenham girls go on to university, with dreams of becoming doctors, lawyers and lecturers. Presumably, they are *all* getting the National Curriculum's required maths and science.

Which way forward with this problem of male bias in schools?

Women can manipulate the National Curriculum to counteract male bias. It says right there that equal opportunities for all pupils 'should permeate every aspect of the curriculum'. It says right there that 'schools need to foster a climate in which equality of opportunity is supported by a policy to which the whole school subscribes'. So let's get creative, says Pat Mahony (1992). Let's use the National Curriculum to provide ' a decent education for girls [that] would include enabling them to grasp the continuum and mechanisms of male dominance and the strategies women have used past and present to resist'.

Why not, in teaching modern languages, have students compare what sports women and men play in different countries and the reasons used when women are excluded? In personal, social and health education, why not have students discuss how the social classes in society are maintained? And in home economics, why not study who produces and prepares food in the world (women) and who controls its unequal distribution (men)?

And when a school decides that single-sex groupings work better for girls in technology and the physical sciences, make sure girls-only classes are offered *not* to make girls as good as 'boys naturally are', but are presented as an antidote to the ways boys behave in mixed-sex classrooms.

The woman you will meet in the next chapter illustrates the way male bias worked just a few decades ago. Teresa Davis was educated at an upper-class boarding-school geared towards the arts. She had such poor maths instruction she barely passed maths O-level, and she learned no science at all. Her brother, who went to Eton, got mathematics and science whether he wanted them or not. Fortunately, Teresa's daughter's school 'aims to produce women who are able to speak for themselves and participate fully in life'.

Chapter 15

Teresa Davis   *From Piano Teacher to Cytogeneticist*

The OU means standing on my own feet for the first time. There are lots of areas in me I'd like to change which haven't yet, but there are very important areas which have changed. It's giving things a try and not being frightened of responsibility. I had the big responsibility of a child, as a single parent, but once a child is there, you just get on with it. But I was always frightened of a job that might lead to problems if anything went wrong. I'd hardly looked down a microscope, but the OU gave me the confidence to learn new techniques and to be part of a responsible team.

Guy's Hospital was the setting in which Teresa Davis stood on her own feet for the first time. True, she had worked for many years as a piano teacher, but teaching children became, for Teresa, too difficult, so she switched to teaching adults. And giving lessons at home is a far cry from joining the throngs surging up in the lifts of this vast institution where an entire floor is devoted to 'Conservative Dental Surgery'.

We met for our second interview at her bench in Genetic Counselling. I set my tape recorder beside her microscope and we pushed aside a box of slides to make room for our tea mugs. It was after 5 o'clock and her colleagues were finishing up their work and calling 'Goodnight' as we began.

Teresa is slender, petite, has short straight brown hair, and wears little if any make-up over her delicate features. She was comfortable in trousers, blouse and sweater both times we met. The first time she gave me tea was at an ancient wooden table in her low-ceilinged kitchen on the ground floor of her big house in Stockwell. Daughter Alice came down to shake my hand and take away a snack of Marmite and toast.

Teresa's potted history in her letter to me read:

> Born in 1946, I was educated at a boarding-school geared towards the arts. I left school with 7 GCEs, studied the piano and took an LRAM, taught piano, married, had one daughter and started my OU degree in 1980. I took a long time over it, enjoying enormously the opportunity to study new subjects, particularly chemistry. I collected my 1st Class Honours Degree at Ely in 1990 and started work as a cytogeneticist at Guy's Hospital in September 1990. My daughter is now seventeen and I have been a single parent for ten years, so my new career offers an exciting future at a time when many people have to face a rather bleak transition.

Would you elaborate a little more about your career as a piano teacher?

I studied piano from the age of 5, but my training started in earnest after abandoning A-levels. I began in 1966 at the age of 20 and I had a wonderful teacher at the Royal Academy of Music. After four years I did a licentiate (LRAM), which qualified me as a teacher. I went on having lessons for another four years and taught children until my daughter was born, which was in 1973. Then I gave it up because it was very difficult to teach with an infant in the house. I took it up again gradually, teaching adults when she went to school, and did some voluntary work at the state school where she went. When she was seven and about to move school, my marriage split up and I needed to earn. So they employed me there and I increased my teaching. I started doing OU courses when she was rising three, but I got ready with a preparatory course through the National Extension College for which you had to write the odd essay and I read books on studying and organizing one's time.

What were your reasons for studying with the OU?

There were tremendous divisions in education when I was in school. Unless you went to exceptionally good girls' schools, you wouldn't get the education that boys got. Consequently, I was really worried about my lack of education, I was ashamed of it. The man I was married to was very encouraging. He didn't say, 'You are uneducated. You should do something about it.' He said he would do everything to make it as easy as possible. He had a degree, he was very bright, very quick, and much more educated than I was. The men I met were generally much more educated. I remember one man in particular looking aghast that I hadn't heard of Smuts or didn't know about some battle, and I felt very, very small.

So my original motivation for the OU was to learn about the world and how things worked. But my life changed while I was studying. I had a marriage, and then I didn't have a marriage. I didn't need a job, and then I did. My life didn't go the way I thought it was going to go at all. So my objectives with the OU changed.

What obstacles to studying with the OU did you have?

I was brought up in an upper-middle-class home. My father worked for the War Office. He died when I was nine. That's probably why I had a rotten education, because my mother wasn't very interested in girls being educated. I've got a sister who is six years older who is a ballet dancer and she also didn't have an academic education at all. And I have a brother who is two years younger and went to Eton and had an excellent education.

I felt very angry about it because I always loved maths, and my father was interested in maths and we used to play mathematical games. I went to two boarding-schools and there was a maths teacher the first term, but after that there was no maths teacher. At my next school, we had a lovely lady, but she couldn't teach maths to save her life. Only four of us took O-level maths and I was the only one who passed. I felt very cross about this because my brother was at prep school in Kent and he never did any work. So these two people used to come to tutor him in the holidays. They used to talk to me about maths. I was so envious. Oh, I longed to be sent to that boys' prep school.

In spite of this, when I left school I wanted to do medicine. I'd been told my father had been interested in medicine and from the age of 13 until I was 17 I had a total crush, an utter obsession, with our local GP. I was looking for a father figure and latched onto this doctor, spending many hours trying to catch a glimpse of him. I hardly knew what it meant to be a doctor but what I did know was that I had none of the subjects needed to do medicine. So I went to a crammer in Notting Hill Gate and tried to cram for physics, chemistry, and biology at A-level, having not done any physics or chemistry, ever. And I was with students who had not only done O-levels, but had failed A-levels. I was right out of my depth. But what sticks in my mind was they told me that the reason I didn't understand physics was because I was no good at maths. This was a terrible knock to my pride. If my maths is no good, I thought, then nothing's any good, and that's the end of it.

What does the OU mean to you?

It's strangely hard to answer. But when you say Open University to me, I feel everything wanting to smile. It's brightened my life. I find it a very exciting idea. I think being educated is the most exciting thing in the world. I want to study forever. It's only because I'm really busy at the moment and extremely stretched that I'm not trying to do something else. I've wakened up. My brain worked so slowly before and now it is much sharper. I see everything in a slightly different way. If I were a bred in the bones scientist, I would have been at it earlier. But even now, learning to look at things in a scientific way changes your life.

Tell me about the OU and its impact on your career.

Well, I just wouldn't have my job if I hadn't got a science degree. So in terms of hours per week, that's an enormous impact, isn't it, and it finances me as well. I always felt slightly bad that I didn't work full-time, and that it was high time I got up and got on with things like other people. It makes me feel a bit more decent to be working quite long hours. I do work hard and it's good for me. Piano teaching I loved, and I liked the pupils very much, but that was pleasurable in a different way. This is more gritty, there is a very different feel to the work.

People used to say, 'Are you going to get a job? Are you going to go into research?' And I used to say, 'Well, I might.' But really I used to say that because people acted as though I oughtn't to be spending all this time with the OU if I wasn't going to do something in the future. But perhaps I'm somebody who lives in the present rather. My daughter wasn't at the age where I wanted to work full-time. I wanted to be free in the holidays for her and obviously a career like the one I've got now wouldn't fit in with that. So I purposely didn't look too far ahead. I got my head down and thought, I'll just get on with what I've got to do at the moment. My piano teaching had gradually increased, the money had gradually increased. It was all ticking over nicely and I didn't want to upset the applecart.

Chemistry and maths wouldn't seem to have anything to do with music, but did your OU studies affect your music teaching career in any way?

The link between the two was in my confidence. My confidence in the years before Alice went off to school was at a fairly low ebb. I felt pretty much chained to the home and to nappies. And pretty fast asleep in my head. So it had this wonderful waking-up effect on me and made me able to say that I wanted to find pupils. Somebody said, 'I wish you'd give me some lessons' and somebody else said, 'I wish you'd give me some lessons.' And I found somewhere to advertise. And it gradually built up. I had 18 to 20 people, one lesson a week.

How do you see work differently now?

I feel successful now because I'm enjoying life, all the opportunities it's bringing, all the excitement and newness I'm feeling. If I were made redundant – and looking for jobs is terrifying, not a thought I relish – I'm not someone who would do nothing. I'd get another job. It would be appalling to be in a world where there was nothing I could do. I think I'd cope with it well. If I couldn't get a job in science, I'd get something. Quite a contrast to my mother. It doesn't occur to her that women work. Just as it didn't seem important that I should have an education. She's never worked, her money's inherited, she's never had to earn a penny. It wouldn't occur to her that I would work for money.

What is the most important use you make of your OU degree?

My job. After I got my degree, I felt quite low. I had to get a job. I had to find something to fill that space in my life that the OU had filled.

What was I then? I was 43. I thought I've got to have a go if I'm going to use this degree. If it doesn't work out, I've got something else I can do, teaching piano. I didn't know where to start. I got a newspaper from the OU about some convention of people offering jobs to graduates. So I wandered over to this hotel in Hammersmith, and I looked at anything that had to do with chemistry, the Met forensic labs and one or two petroleum companies, Sainsbury's and I applied to all of those. The only interview I got was with the forensic lot and that was most alarming. I was cross-questioned on chemistry for an hour by a board of three crusty men. And they didn't offer me a job because I had no experience.

Then I met two people at choir practice one evening, both linked with genetics. I had done a genetics course and had always been interested in genetics, but I hadn't thought that I could get into genetics because my degree was mainly chemistry and maths. One person said, 'I work in cytogenetics at Guy's and we are looking for people,' and the other was married to a geneticist at Guy's, so both of them in the end led me to the same department. Eventually I had an interview and they offered me the job. They wanted somebody with a science degree and it didn't matter what the science degree was, just the discipline of having done it.

What are some examples of transfers from your studies to your job?

The first-year science foundation course, we had various different teachers because there were different disciplines and they were helpful. But meeting other students, usually that was the most important thing, because from fairly early on I realized, Well, I have to jump in at the deep end and ask other people how they were getting on, and if they felt like getting together and discussing it. That's what you lack at the OU that you normally get in a conventional university where people sit around at coffee time and talk about the meaning of this and that. Meeting as a group was tremendously helpful. We spent a lot of time studying at my kitchen table.

And that has transferred to working. It's opened up a great opportunity of making friends and being exposed to a whole group of new people. And if you're with new people, you're having to learn ways to cope with them and communicate with them. I've never been in a hierarchy before, where I have a boss and there's somebody above that, and somebody above that. It's an extraordinary thing to experience at my age. I'm at the bottom of the pack with a lot of young people and it makes me feel younger, quite invigorated.

So the OU made me more articulate and if I feel strongly about something, I'm much more able to say what I think without getting into a panic. If I'm having difficulty communicating with somebody, I go away and think, Now this is what I really want to say, and this is how I need to overcome this difficulty, and then I approach them and with a bit of luck and the confidence, I'm able to transmit it in a reasonable form. The OU brought me here in the first place, and then coping with things gives me more confidence.

Why was the OU right for you?
I was shy at pitching in, afraid of failing. That's why it was right for me. Because I could fail by myself quietly with nobody seeing me, if necessary. So I dared to do it. Having been to this crammer where I couldn't keep up, I didn't want to put myself in that position again. Basically, there's nothing to lose. You're competing against yourself.

How did you balance your OU studies with your family and piano teaching?
I'd do my studying as much as I could in the daytime and any more that I needed to do I did after Alice had gone to bed. It was part of her life right from the beginning, so she thought it was quite normal. Later on I studied when she was doing her homework, so that was good. She's very industrious, but she doesn't enjoy it as much as I do. I don't think she thinks, Wonderful, now I can get down to studying, like I did. She's more sensible. I'm compulsive and she's more normal. She's doing her A-levels now in geography, art history and biology, and she wants to go to university and study anthropology after a year working in Nepal.

In contrast to my boarding-school experiences, Alice's school aims to produce women who are able to speak for themselves and participate fully in life. She has surprised me all the way along with her ability to be some of the things I've always wanted to be, like being able to step back and weigh things up. So many parents want their children to follow in their footsteps; I'd like to be more like her.

What is the most important ingredient in women-in-general's success at the OU?
I wouldn't advise them to do it if they don't like working hard and if they find it hard working on their own. Some people find it hard working on their own and you have to do a lot of that and you have to have the time. I particularly feel that people who are retiring – my next degree will be when I retire – for them it's absolutely to be recommended. What a wonderful thing to do in your seventies.

What was the hardest part of study? The easiest?

That first foundation course in science was pitched at just the right level. The material was hard to grasp, but enough was possible so that it was exciting to be able to learn anything. The units were written at the right level, there were good feedback questions and background reading. My three tutors were very helpful, although at this stage I was too beset by adolescent fears to ask questions. Physics was a shattering experience. We had to work out a figure for the acceleration due to gravity by dropping things down from the top of the staircase, timing with a stopwatch, and rolling things down inclined planes, hours and hours of dropping things and timing and then we had to write this experiment up using two great books, one about writing up experiments and one about the mathematics behind experiments. It took me at least 24 hours to write that first TMA question. But it came back with a good mark and I was very pleased, but I thought I can't always spend this much time on one question. By the end of that course, I was still spending 24 hours on a TMA but I was used to it by then.

The tutorials in the higher-up courses were wonderful; they were much smaller, and we had some very good tutors at the higher-level courses. Apart from one unpleasant man, I never heard a tutor put anybody down and they had some very tricky people, who they managed very well. Certainly the best meetings were when you felt you could join in and ask questions, but sometimes they just had to steam ahead.

I took the science foundation course and maths foundation course, physiology, genetics, the biological basis of behaviour, organic chemistry, inorganic chemistry, pure maths second-level course, physics, physical chemistry, a general chemistry course, and a fourth-level science course which was really your own project on a particular brand of a particular drug. Obviously the practical side of studying chemistry by correspondence is limited so that the summer schools are very, very intensive. I did one every year except for one year, most at Nottingham.

What advantage is there in OU studies versus a conventional university?

I came from a very narrow middle-class background where you didn't meet anybody outside your own social sphere. So going to OU tutorials and summer schools and meeting up with all these different sorts of people, yes, it's enormously broadening. I don't think I ever thought that people from one class were better than people of another class because my nanny was from a working-class background and she was the best person I knew. But the OU gave me the opportunity to meet lots of new people and to have relationships with men from different backgrounds. I recently broke up with a man from a different background and it's been one of the saddest things that's ever happened to me. I felt he was too controlling and not able to let me be an individual, and he would say that that was untrue and that I was trying to prove I was above him by wanting to be an individual. I was fighting for my freedom, just trying to be equal, and he was fighting what he took to be class dominance in me.

To what do you attribute your success with the OU?

Great determination. If I really want to understand something, I just go on until I do. My goodness, I worked. I've got a reasonable sort of brain; it's not fast; in fact, I'm quite a slow learner. No, it's just perseverance and enjoyment. All the people I worked with were very hard-working. Lots of them had full-time jobs and four children and a husband who didn't want them to do it, all that stuff, and doing three courses at once.

Tell me about your job and what your career plans are.

My job is to culture cells. We do a lot of cell culturing for foetuses that aren't developing normally. Our patients are pregnant women with pregnancies that aren't going well, men and women who have been trying to have children and aren't conceiving, girls and boys who don't go into puberty at a sensible sort of time. Or babies that are born that don't look normal. We culture cells and we then have to make slides of them and then we have to stain them and do various processes to them, then look down the microscope and analyse the chromosomes and report back. Guy's is a very big genetic centre, we're the Southeast Regional Genetic Centre. Occasionally I get a little project that is research-based, but it's definitely a clinical job.

It was very exciting to find the first little bit of chromosome that was missing, that was quite small and difficult to see. And people were very nice to me and said that it was really hard to see and that was wonderful. Of course, I'm meant to see everything that's not right.

I could go on doing what I'm doing and move up the ladder and have more responsibility. Another possibility would be to move into research, say in three years' time, which is less sure. Research is on a nine-month contract, or two-year contract. If I were confident enough about job changes, I might do that. I've got this friend whose husband has a cytogenetics institute in Sardinia. And he has suggested that I work there for a bit. But the natural progression would be to finish training, pass the official qualifying exam for the Association of Clinical Cytogeneticists, and move into more senior work. You have to know the job inside out first, so you don't study for the exam until you've had 2 to 3 years of experience. It would suit me best to start studying when Alice is at university.

What was most important in your life before the OU and now?

My family life, Alice. And Alice is still the most important thing – if there were something drastically wrong with her I would stop working. But I was very aware that Alice is not going to be around much longer and that other things will get more important, like my friends and gardening. What's changed is that I've got a job which is also very important. That's a shock to the system. It was exhausting to start with, but I feel I'm in the right place.

At the very end of our second interview, Teresa explained to me that when she was little she saw her mother for only a quarter of an hour at the end of the day, looking and smelling wonderful, and that was it. The person she really got to know as a child was her nanny, named Alice. This woman had looked after Teresa's mother and her seven sisters and at the age of 60 began raising Teresa.

What was she like, your first Alice?

She was practical, warm, loving, gentle, but very old-fashioned in that she didn't encourage children to explore. So she was restrictive at the same time that she was calm and very good at listening. She had patience and extraordinary adaptability. She was genuinely happy giving her whole life to other people's children. She died 14 years ago, having come to live with us in Stockwell, so she was here when my Alice was born. And they had a lovely, though brief, relationship.

———————————

Gloria Steinem was in town and I was carrying around with me a review of her latest book, which has to do with self-exploration, and I gave it to Teresa as we parted. Teresa's on a quest to continue to change herself, to be what? More patient and adaptable, like the first Alice? Better able to step back and weigh things up, like the second Alice? The thing is, the OU was the catalyst for Teresa changing and for her exciting future.

Chapter 16

Lack of Emotional Support

Clare Bardsley, aged 46, picked up an upper second in organization studies with English after five years of study. 'I found fitting part-time study around a full-time job very difficult in the first year,' she said. 'But you do – you have to. My husband used to do all the washing and ironing. He used to ask me what I would do if I wasn't doing a degree.' Mr Bardsley died 18 months ago. 'Because he was so sympathetic, I decided to continue with the course. He gave me the final drive to complete it.' (Ward, 1992)

Ordinary women become extraordinary women with a little help from their friends and family. 'Like most women, if people hadn't pushed me, I wouldn't have done it,' Margaret Beckett, MP and deputy leader of the Labour Party, confided in her interview with Lesley White in 1992. Starting with her teacher mother and carpenter father, Beckett was given strong emotional support to get a first-rate education and a significant career. Today her husband, Leo Beckett, provides that emotional support in addition to managing her office and protecting her time.

But how many women *don't* get a positive push from their families when they step out of the homemaker role to go back to school? Too many get total lack of interest, says Anne Garner (1990), or worse, children and husbands who make home life 'as minimally conducive to study as is possible'.

One story I heard while interviewing was of a woman who quit the OU for a full decade when her husband turned violent because of her studies. He had wanted her at home all day, 'doing things for the children', but at the same time taunted her lack of schooling and demanded that she do something about it. His method was to read books at home, alone. So she began reading at home alone, but when she tried to discuss her reading with him, he'd explode, 'That's bloody stupid, you've got the whole wrong end of it.' If she tried studying at weekends, there would be a big argument. Finally, as her OU education progressed, he became physically threatening. So she quit for ten whole years until he left her for a younger woman and she could start again.

How does lack of emotional support for women's education affect us as girls?

If parents do not encourage it, girls are not likely to develop a serious interest in education. Arlene McLaren (1985) described 48 women in a residential adult education college who had been out of education for many years. They remembered being unhappy at school whether it was a village school or a secondary modern or a grammar school or whether they had come from a privileged background. Many had left school at 14, 15, the majority at 16. Some had no qualifications at all. A common theme in their recollections was not being encouraged by their parents to pursue an education. Their parents made absolutely no effort to help them do well in school and expected them to get a job in an office and then get married, that was it.

For many working-class girls, on top of parental lack of interest, the typical co-educational comprehensive is most unwelcoming (Thompson, 1983a). Non-academic, working-class and black girls, especially, are seen by teachers to 'voluntarily choose' girls' subjects and later choose girls' jobs only as a temporary diversion before getting married. Thompson, a lecturer in adult education at the University of Southampton's 'Second Chance for Women,' uses the women's words to convey how unpleasant and meaningless school was to them: 'The teachers did not seem to care whether you understood what they said.' 'There never seemed to be much effort put into the actual enjoyment level of the pupils.' 'I left school at the age of 15 with no qualifications, labelled by the teachers as "factory fodder".'

Isn't it the teachers' role not only to lend girls their emotional support but to get their parents involved and provide encouragement as well? Hymas and Nelson (1992) found girls from an East End 'pocket of social deprivation' attending a girls-only school where 30 per cent of them gained five or more GCSE A to C grades. Even though English was the second language of 97 per cent of the girls in the fifth year, more than three-quarters achieved at least one GCSE at grades A to C! The biggest reason for this success? The strong link forged between the school and the parents. 'High expectations' and 'good relations with parents' were the reasons for 80 per cent of the girls in this school of 1,360 pupils continuing their studies after 16.

How does lack of emotional support for education affect adult women?

Husbands and children who would rather Mum stay home are aided and abetted by the men who draw up the curricula of the Workers' Educational Association (WEA) and local education authorities (LEAs). These men show an amazing consensus about what women want – classes in cookery, child development, keep fit, and make-up and beauty. These authorities think the only reason why a woman seeks further education is to get out of the house for a while and for the company of others. These guys have a difficult time with the concept that women want courses that meet their needs for self-fulfilment (Thompson, 1983b).

Women outnumber men in LEA provision by 3 to 1, and in university and WEA provision by 2 to 1. But as long as what is a 'relevant' curriculum is defined by men, it won't reflect women's experiences and expectations.

Helen Seddon, whose story comes next, thinks one reason why she failed A-levels was that her parents didn't expect her to be particularly good at anything, and she assumed she wasn't bright because she always came at the bottom of the class. Her mother had a very negative childhood and even now 'doesn't expect anything good to happen'. Helen believes that her father would have been happier if he felt he could express his feelings and not forever have to be a man in a man's world. Helen's expectations of herself were pretty low until, to her amazement, she passed her first OU arts foundation exam. Then nothing could keep her new expectations of herself from being fulfilled.

Chapter 17

Helen Seddon   *From Senior Law Clerk to What?*

I do feel much, much happier about myself. I'm almost to the point where I'm afraid of going over the top, I'm so enthusiastic. I've been thinking back how I enjoyed learning new things and I could do that in a new job. On the other hand, I can carry on doing this job, carry on making my boss think I'm worth having. Last week when I was off skiing, another girl joined and she left within a week and her name was Helen. Someone came to his door and said, 'Sir, Helen's resigned.' And he went, 'My God, no!' Everyone's been telling me how he reacted because he thought it was me.

Helen and I met twice in her office, 'The Cooperage,' several bustling streets east of London Bridge station.

Helen is petite, pretty with bouncy brown curls, and dresses fashionably. Her manner was cordial and assured as she showed me into her boss's office after her colleagues had waved their farewells on the way to a nearby pub. Her evening classes in painting and French are balanced by the fact that she is an experienced downhill skier.

Helen was born in 1953, was 38 when we first met, and had worked for twenty years since leaving school, first for the Metropolitan Police and then for the Crown Prosecution Service (CPS), moving up from office worker to Senior Law Clerk. She has never been married but lived for seven years with a partner. They have ended their relationship and she has bought out his share of their house in Eltham Park. Her OU studies lasted from 1983 until 1989. She took a year off from the OU 'to reflect', but ended up using it to read the books for her next course on the nineteenth-century novel.

Helen's father was a police sergeant. After her four children were off to school, her mother worked for the police in one of their typing units.

What were your reasons for pursuing an OU degree?

I started work at 18 as a clerical officer for the Metropolitan Police solicitor's department for which I needed only four O-levels. When I got to work, I realized I wasn't as thick as I thought I was. I got promoted quite quickly. In two and a half years I got promoted to the next grade, Executive Officer. Next comes Higher Executive Officer. And I got to my present grade when I was 26, which is quite good going. But once I'd achieved what I thought was the highest I would ever go, I thought, I've done it, I'm going to be bored now. What's there to go for? That's when I started to think about the OU degree and started it when I was 29, three years later, in 1983.

All my friends had degrees and I thought, I want one of those. And my boyfriend, somebody I'd known since school, he'd got a degree, was working on his MSc and went on to do a PhD. I thought, I don't see how he can like me if I haven't got a degree.

In the arts foundation course, I remember thinking, There's a cut-off, so try it out, and if I get this far, I'll be happy. And then I thought, If I get to summer school, I'll be happy. And then, If I get to the end, I'll be happy. And then, well, it doesn't matter if I pass the exam because I've achieved a year's constant study. Which I had never done before. So when I got through the first year and passed the exam, I really thought I had achieved something. I had a self-image of never succeeding at anything academic, so I thought, Gosh, I *can* do it and then I carried on.

I wanted to be able to look at everything around me in a more informed, analytical and educated way, so I did mainly arts courses. I'd hear people going to a play and they would be analysing it and I'd think, I never thought of it like that. And it makes me happy now that I can walk around London and look at the architecture and I know its history.

What obstacles did you have to overcome?
Well, I passed my 11-plus, to everybody's surprise, and went to a co-ed local grammar school in New Cross in south London but I didn't do very well. I ended up with four O-levels: English language, English literature, art, religious knowledge. I stayed on to do A-levels but failed them, English lit and economic history. I don't think my parents expected me to be any good at anything. So I didn't have any great expectations of myself.

The school that I went to, in the first year, when you're eleven, you went in alphabetically; the classes were divided 30 to each class, starting from A to Z. In the second year, following the exams, we were streamed; the best ten from each class formed the A stream. And the remaining two classes were alphabetical. The A stream studied Latin, the Bs didn't. The As were also pinpointed as achievers. I did try hard in my junior school and passed my 11-plus, but somehow I always came in the bottom five or ten. I came to accept that I couldn't do any better. The reason I failed my A-levels is I didn't do any work. I assumed I wasn't bright. It was proved to me every year. When I think about it now, why ever would I have taken the A-level economic history? I probably liked the sound of the words. English literature was natural for me to do, it was the only thing I was consistently able at.

I don't think the school would have wanted it thought that boys did science and girls did English, but that was the pattern it followed. In the first two years everybody did general science and I did fine. But third and fourth years it was chemistry, biology and physics. I honestly don't know if I consciously thought I can't do physics because I'm a girl, or what. But there's no doubt about it: most boys did physics and chemistry and maths for their A-levels, and most girls did biology.

So as far as obstacles to studying with the OU, with this self-image of not being good at anything academic, the only obstacle would have been myself.

I started the OU when I was 29. Three years into my degree, my next sister started a full-time degree at Thames Polytechnic. She graduated the same year as me. My brother, five years younger, just got a social work qualification at Reading University. And my sister who is nine years younger than me is in her second year of a degree at Thames Polytechnic. So we all started late, but I'm sure my OU degree set them all thinking.

Tell me more about your parents' attitudes.

Mum had a very negative childhood. She was the second of five. I always remember her saying that her mother didn't like girls. She was brought up by her grandmother from about the age of 5. And when the war started, she was evacuated from one town in Wales to another, moving from one aunt to another. So she was brought up by a succession of aunts. She said to me, 'I never asked for anything because I knew no one would ever hear me.' Mum doesn't expect anything good to happen, she was so deprived.

Her normal reaction when I say, 'Mum, I'm going to go somewhere and do something', will be, 'What, all the way there?' I'm nearly forty and I'm still having this. But whereas she will say, 'Oh, my God, you're not going to do that', and it's fear, Dad has the opposite view of things.

I went to Kenya a couple of years ago. That's really exciting, isn't it? A good thing to do. And I was expressing my excitement and I was starting to become afraid, and Dad said to me, 'Ahh, it's just a lump of dirt. What are you worried about?'

As a policeman, my Dad was quite unusual. Bit of a square peg in a round hole. He was the one who read the *Guardian*. He's 67 now and he stills talks about the war. About going into the Air Force at 18, having to learn how to be a man, having to control your feelings, be on top of your emotions. His advice was always, 'Never let anybody see how you feel. Self-control is all.'

After the war, my Dad had the chance to stay in the Air Force, go into teaching, or join the police force. I think he would have been better as a teacher. He would have been a more comfortable person for the rest of his life if he hadn't been burdened by forever having to be a man in a man's world.

What does the OU mean to you?

It's a chance for people to further their education without having to go through the process of proving yourself first by having so many A-levels. It's open for everybody and it opened lots of mental doors for me.

We had to do two foundation courses, so I did the social sciences foundation course next, and I got a distinction in that. I stuck it on the wall, it was such a confidence booster. I couldn't believe it was me that got this academic success even though it's not the highest standard. And I thought then, This must be my area because I got As all the way through. So I did a second-level sociology course but I didn't enjoy it. I thought, Why am I doing this? But then I had become quite obsessed with OU and had a real fear of failing. I'd gone from being pleased to get through the first year to being obsessed with getting a degree.

The tutor would say to me, 'Just write what you think,' but I was very stuck to the units and afraid to move away from them. I didn't have confidence in my own understanding. Every essay that I ever wrote for the OU was the same trauma.

I had basically reasonable attitudes about things, but they developed and now I understand more about what's going on; monetarism, living in a pluralist political system.

And it gave me a feeling of wider ability to appreciate the things that I enjoy, like literature and art and theatre.

What does a senior law clerk do? And what impacts has your OU degree had on your career?

The job's changed over the years. Senior law clerks used to read cases and draft indictments. It was a fairly intellectual exercise. You'd be reading the statements in a case and you'd be deciding on what charges were appropriate and you'd be drafting them. Before CPS the road to promotion was showing that you knew the criminal law. There was also a management function at that time, basically responsible for almost everything that went on in the office in partnership with the principal. Since the CPS it has changed quite a lot. When it became a national system, people looked at it and thought, Well, we've got to have lawyers doing this, so now lawyers draft charges.

The law clerks, which is what I am, prepare cases for the Crown Court, for the trial, but the charges have already been decided by the lawyers. We look at the cases and ask for any further evidence which needs to be obtained. I work in a section of law clerks. I think we have got 45 staff here, who are responsible for making sure that all cases which are committed for trial are ready for trial, all the evidence has been obtained, all the procedural matters have been resolved. My boss also deals with the personnel management side of the job, so it has become far less legal, and it was the legal side that I preferred.

When the whole prosecution service in the country was nationalized and all the independent services came under one umbrella in 1986, which is the CPS, I was about half-way through the OU. First, I was offered a temporary promotion to the next grade, which would have been long-term. But I turned it down. I didn't want more pressure from my job pushing OU out of the way. And when the CPS started, I applied for promotion simply because it was absolutely the expected thing to do. I couldn't handle everybody saying, 'But you *must* want promotion. Think of the money.' But for the second time, I thought that the pressures of that job would be too much, so I withdrew. I didn't want to give the OU up. It was my target for proving myself.

But I was also afraid of the next step up. I was afraid that I couldn't cope with it. You are the one who answers for the section. I've done it on a temporary basis so I know I can do it. But in the past I thought, All these people think I'm capable, but they're wrong, I'm not really.

Also I couldn't argue against part of the fear being one woman amongst a lot of men. There are women in the next grade up. But there are no women in my area above the grade above me. A friend of mine who is a grade above me goes to these high-level meetings and it's all men around her, and they've got a very patronizing attitude. So you do have a double battle on your hands.

So what changes are you contemplating in your career?

There is a scheme where graduates can be sponsored to convert their degree into a law degree and then you do the common practice exam which results in your either being a solicitor or a barrister and being taken on as a crown prosecutor. I haven't done it yet, basically because I haven't wanted to do any more studying of that intensity. I needed to rest from it. I wouldn't have to work at the same time though, so it might sound ridiculous that I haven't done it. Essentially it's doing a three-year law degree in one year. I would need as much energy to embark on that as I needed to do OU and work at the same time. It's a very intense course and I would be sponsored and be under pressure to succeed because I was being paid for, pay, fees and everything.

Also recently I had a career interview. But it's not something that you come away from thinking, Oh, good, my career's going to start moving now. It's like filling in an application form for the OU, something might come up in a couple of years' time. But now they know who I am, and they know I am looking for something new, and sometimes when jobs come up or a new department is created, they will go to this section and say, 'Is there anyone around who is looking for something new? Have you got anybody good?' So if I hadn't gone to them, they wouldn't have known about me. My degree can only go in my favour, but you have to wait in the Civil Service for an opportunity to arise. You don't just get promoted.

If I do go back to class, I will associate with women with backgrounds closer to mine. Because there is a difference. You can't help being aware of it, can you? You've only got to walk into an English courtroom to be aware of the class system. The judge is sitting up there, he speaks in one accent. The solicitors and the people like me are sitting in the middle and we speak with another accent, and the prisoners are at the back and they speak with a different accent. From the day I left school and walked into a crown court, I saw it. There's somebody in the office who comes from south-east London, the same as I do, and if we're in a pub and we start laughing, something about south-east London and where the c's and h's go, our accent changes again. And if I'm at court and talking to barristers, I'm conscious of the fact that I pronounce my words differently for them. Graduates who come in here from universities, they go into court for the first time, and there are all these people talking in these different accents, and they hate it. They've never come across it before.

Do you use your OU degree in your job?

Yes, not the content of what I learned, but my approach to work. Apart from the fact that I felt a lot more confident to express my opinions and felt better about myself, I had a far more analytical approach from the techniques I acquired at the OU. Everything I did was of a higher quality. I got on really well with my boss at the time, who I quite admired for his intellectual capabilities. We were on a similar wavelength so we could discuss work in an informed, intelligent way. He used to read all my OU essays as well, because he was interested. I really had a surge of confidence about the third year when I realized I could do it. I started off not knowing that much about a particular area to being in a position where I'd go to him and say, 'I think X, Y, Z,' and he'd said, 'You do?' And he hadn't thought of it.

Were there any transfers from your liberal arts studies to your job?

We would write what we call instructions to counsel, a brief. And my composition in my instructions to counsel and my language skills improved through doing the degree. I would make it a far more structured document than I had done before. I would look at it and think, Now I'm setting out what I'm going to say, and now I'm saying it, and now I'm concluding it. This particular boss quite admired my writing, he used to say things like he enjoyed reading my briefs because they were something interesting to read rather than a bald set of facts put together without any real structure. I also worked with someone who had a degree in classics and we both enjoyed words and composing interesting reading for the barristers.

How did you balance your OU studies with your job and the rest of life?

I used to study on the train going to work and coming home. And I used to feel that as long as I'd done an hour a day, minimum, that I could keep pace with the units. It became part of my life. If I had an essay to write, then I'd give up the whole weekend. And starting the OU coincided with the starting of a relationship. We bought a house. I started OU in February 1983, I moved into the house with my partner in December 1983. We decided it was going to be a permanent relationship.

It all kind of fitted in together and he was at college doing his doctorate so it seemed quite good that we both had studying to do. He was very supportive in lots of ways. I did have a social life but I never had any time to myself. I never left my house to go anywhere in the car without my OU unit with me. If I had to wait two hours for the RAC to come round and didn't have my units with me, I'd have been so frustrated. I lived it really. But I never gave myself any space and I don't think that was particularly healthy.

Why would you advise women today to get an OU degree?

It depends on your personal circumstances and on how much you are willing to give up. I have a big mortgage now on my own, so I couldn't finance an ordinary degree. I could sell the house and live in student accommodation, but I didn't want to do that then, and I wouldn't want to do it now. The OU allows one to do both things: it allows you to carry on with the career that you've got and study at the same time. And women who are at home or work part-time can also do OU, and I feel I could advise anyone to do OU if they were interested in studying in that way. But you have to have the basic will and be prepared to study at home. I chose it because I didn't think I had the staying power to go to evening classes two or three nights a week to do a degree after work. That's one of the overriding features of the OU. You choose your time, you study when you want to, when it's convenient to you.

Tell me what was the hardest and easiest part of OU study.

The easiest, the most enjoyable, was summer school. I craved someone who wanted to listen to me going on about whatever subject I happened to be studying. When you're working or in a partnership, you're surrounded by people who aren't going to respond in the way that you want them to respond. At summer school everybody felt the same. I did two foundation summer schools, I went to Stirling in Scotland and I went to Sussex for the social science. And I did the nineteenth-century novel course at York.

So it was a release of all the pent-up desire to talk about the course. You spend a whole week talking non-stop, which is a good, satisfying thing to do. I wasn't in and out of people's bedrooms. That's one of the famous ideas people have about summer schools. I wasn't aware of anything like that, to be honest. For the nineteenth-century novel course we had a tutor whom I could imagine I could have fallen in love with, and I went home and told my partner and he said, 'You can see how students fall in love with their lecturers, can't you?' I went to the discos, the bar, everything, but I wasn't looking for romance.

The biggest drawback is not having people to talk to on a day-to-day basis. I always wanted to know how other people were doing, but people didn't always want to tell you what their grades were. I went to all the tutorials but it wasn't the same as summer school. It was hard to get people interested in self-help groups. The one I went to was good, but it's another night out.

What quality about you made you succeed with the OU?

I never realized that I could do something for so long and so persistently. Discovering that in the beginning made me carry on. Things that I knew nothing about became interesting through the OU. What really kept me going was this idea that I would have proved myself to myself if I got a degree. And I probably chose the hardest way there was to get one. So that made it even more of a proving ground. I'm sure it's easier to go to college when you're 18, study for three years, and come out with a degree.

What was most important before and after the OU?

Pre-OU I was a young, future-ahead-of-me person. My job was quite important, but I'd already achieved what I set out to achieve. The relationship I had with my partner was important. Now? I'm getting myself back together again, recovering from all these years of studying and trying to get over my broken relationship, trying to get my house sorted out, and learning how to be happy. Or learning how not to be unhappy.

It would have been a good thing to have children, but turning 40, I think it's too late now. And that's a shame. But I can do something totally different with my life. I was talking with one of my bosses the other day with whom I talked before about career moves, and he said, 'I was thinking about you the other day, and I think you ought to go for it now.' He meant the law degree. As long as I am in the Civil Service, I can still apply for sponsorship to do that. I've got my 20-odd years behind me with another 20 to go. So that might be the thing to do when I turn 40.

When our second interview ended, Helen dropped me off at London Bridge before joining her mates at the pub. I gave her a Frances Fyfield novel in which the civil servant lawyer heroine is named Helen and I also recommended the play, *Murmuring Judges*, at the Royal National Theatre. I'll bet that when I get in touch with her again, she will have enjoyed both – much more than she would have done, pre-Open University.

Chapter 18

Lack of Financial Support

On my 15th birthday my father said, 'She leaves.' My academic
standard was totally irrelevant. My brothers didn't wish to be
educated further, and therefore neither could I. So I took a crash
course and went to work as a junior stenographer. This was such a
contrast to a senior counsellor I met my first year with the OU. He
had three sons and one daughter but he was only actually paying for
his daughter to go to university. He said the most important
education was his daughter's. A total reversal of everything I'd ever
heard. And he said, 'But the hand that rocks the cradle rules the
world. The better educated the woman is, the better educated the
children are, the better educated the world becomes. It is as simple
as that.' (Jean Posthuma, in conversation, November 1990)

Joyce Nicholson (1980), author of young people's books, described what happened in her
family. Her mother went to the greatest lengths to make Joyce's brother study. Mum
badgered him, waited on him hand and foot, and made great sacrifices for him to go to
university. In contrast, Joyce was constantly told she'd done enough school work and not
to study too hard. At the age of 15, when she tested her parents with the idea of leaving
school and getting a job, her parents encouraged her to leave; they couldn't see any
advantage to her staying at school. But 'had I been a boy any thought of my leaving school
would have been discouraged immediately. I would have been told I must make a career
for myself. I must get better qualifications. And I would have been easily persuaded.'

There are fathers like Joyce Nicholson's still about. Janice's Dad, for example. Janice
passed many GCSEs and was invited to take A-levels. But her father thought, and still
thinks, education is wasted on women and would not support her. So, to stay in school,
Janice got a job at a Tesco supermarket to earn her keep. When she asked her Dad for
money to visit a university in a far-off city, he refused to let her go. She saved her money
and went anyway. Eventually she was offered places at various universities but her father
refused to sign the application for a maintenance grant, again saying, 'Leave school and
get a job.' The county would only give her a grant if she had lived independently of her
parents for three years. So she continues at Tesco's, and Philip Thane (1992), who
recounted her tale, says he is sure she will earn a degree, but will never lead a normal

student life. 'When finally all that hard work pays off, Janice will have her degree and her own private debt mountain. Sad, isn't it?'

And all Janice wanted was her father's signature, not *his* money.

But surely society is compensating for families and funding women's education?

No, says Liz Sperling (1989), financing their studies may be women returners' greatest barrier. Employers won't give women paid education leave to do part-time degrees. The student grant system discriminates against women by giving priority to full-time study done continuously for three years. Local education authorities give low priority to funding traditional women's areas, such as paramedical and arts courses. Women in access courses, Sperling says, have to use their welfare benefits and housekeeping money to pay for the courses, fares, books and childcare expenses.

And what about financing in the future?

> Overall it would seem that the logic behind the introduction of loans and higher fees actually runs counter to what can be expected once they are initiated. Rather than increasing access to higher education, more barriers will have to be traversed. For many women returners this will mean that doors that have previously allowed a few to pass through them will be firmly shut once again. (Sperling, 1989, p. 25)

Because most working-class women need a government grant to attend college, which they only receive after they've been accepted by a college, for some time to come adult students will be women with well-off husbands (McLaren, 1985). What women lack, McLaren says, are the institutionally based, formal types of educational encouragement that men get. Men get release time and financial or promotion incentives from their employers or trade-union organizations.

Men also receive more training in the workplace than women. Using banking as an example, Ann Wickham (1986) cites statistics showing that while 75 per cent of clerical employees were women, only 5 per cent of management, lower and middle, were women. No women were in higher management. This occurs because young women are first placed in secretarial jobs (as men never are), which are not seen as training jobs. And older women are simply not eligible for workplace programmes. Wickham feels the underlying reason for women of all ages being denied internal training is that male bank officials view marriage and children, for women, as incompatible with functioning as a manager.

As for further education – that is, post-school education other than degree-level courses, such as apprenticeships, O- and A-level courses, and training relating to employment – Wickham describes further education as very sex-role stereotyped. There are, literally, men's courses and women's courses, and women don't get non-traditional training opportunities.

Here is what Lynn Hanna (1992) reports from an interview with Joanna Foster, chairwoman of Britain's Equal Opportunities Commission. Foster didn't welcome Britain's opting out of the Social Protocol signed by all the other EC members. It is good news that 90 per cent of new jobs to be created in the next five years will be filled by women. But it's not good news that they will constitute a female sweatshop, an economic underclass of poorly paid part-timers with no rights at all: no rights regarding redundancy, sick pay, holidays *or training*. The hourly rate for women in full-time employment is still 22 per cent lower than that for men. Young women still receive less training than young men. But it is part-time workers, 90 per cent of whom are women, who will be the real losers because the Government has opted out of 'equality between men and women with regard to labour market opportunities and treatment at work'.

Every woman I interviewed remarked spontaneously that she was worried about the rising cost of Open University courses. Not for themselves, they shook their heads, but because so many women are poor, so many can't afford higher education. And without more education, women are trapped permanently in low-paid, unprotected jobs.

Who better to tell you how to hold down a full-time job, raise a family and pay for your college education than Editha Tharpe, who, after her OU degree, is still a nurse but now also a magistrate. Her employer not only gave her no financial support, but also no study days or time off for summer school. Her manager questioned just what this BA she was working on had to do with nursing. She was harassed for studying during the empty hours of night shift and so gave up bringing her books to work. Editha was very concerned that OU courses were getting too high-priced for ordinary women. Tessa Blackstone, Master of Birkbeck College, University of London, expressed a similar concern:

> Part-time students are not eligible for maintenance awards or loans. They pay their own living and travel costs. They buy their own books and pay for extras such as field courses. Because most part-time students have jobs, they contribute to the Exchequer by paying taxes. They are therefore a pretty good deal from the Treasury's point of view. In spite of this, the Treasury insists that part-time students should pay tuition fees on top. In this respect they are discriminated against, since home-based full-time students, however rich they or their parents may be, get free tuition for a first degree. However poor a part-time student is, he or she has to pay. Clearly this is inequitable. (Blackstone, 1992)

The OU women I've met will read this and smile. They'll nod and say, 'Yes, *not having* to pay for a full-time education as a teenager and *having* to pay for a part-time education as an adult is inequitable. But in my case it was worth it!'

Chapter 19

Editha Tharpe *From Nurse to Nurse/Magistrate*

Society used to make women believe that they didn't have too much of an opinion on anything. Society would say, 'That's only a woman talking.' And nursing is the sort of profession where this is how it's done and you go along doing it. You are not encouraged to think for yourself. I was able to break that mould. I learned to say, 'Wait a minute. I've got an opinion.' I found that I would even look critically at the books, which before I thought that the book was the final word. Now I pick up a piece of journalism and, whereas before I would read it and say, 'Well, this is it,' now I might think, Hold on, there is a little hole in this argument.

Editha is a big woman, tall and heavy with a broad, smooth face. In her plain, starched nurse's uniform, with her wavy hair pulled back tightly, and skin the colour of coffee with lots of milk in it, she calls up the image of a living, breathing, non-mythical Earth Mother. She wears no make-up, no jewellery. She moves slowly, deliberately. She speaks reflectively, calmly. 'I'm a Pisces lady. They tell me that you're the world's mother, so I think that's helped a bit. The OU made me much more tolerant of what my children must be going through and I'm much better able to cope with them than if I'd kept my old narrow views where things were black and white.'

Editha, born in 1936 in Jamaica, passed both the Junior Cambridge and Senior Cambridge exams before coming to England in 1955. She started training as a nurse in 1956. She met up again with her husband, with whom she had gone to school in Jamaica, and they married and raised five children, four boys and one girl, together with two other girls who needed a home. In 1990 when Editha and I first met, her children ranged in age from 18 to 29. Her husband was a group station manager for London Underground, while she was a full-time nurse at St Mary Abbots Hospital in Earls Court, where we did both of her interviews. Editha started with the OU in 1977 with A100, the humanities foundation course. She got her bachelor's in 1985, concentrating in sociology. Partly because of her OU studies, Editha has become a lay magistrate.

What were your reasons for studying with the OU?

I went to a job that didn't stretch me enough and I used to read, and I thought I'm reading so much, why don't I put it to study? And it just grew from there. I first approached the Open University because I liked the concept; my children were very small and I was at loose ends with my husband. I felt I was vegetating. The first time I applied, they were oversubscribed and couldn't accept me. But I tried again and was successful.

Basically I wanted to update me, to get confidence, to become a wider person, and I found that. I have not run after another job because I'm doing what I want to do, I like bedside nursing. I don't want management because it's too remote from the bedside. I would recommend the OU to anybody. If a woman finds herself with a child, out of a job, unable to work, I would say to her, 'Go to the Open University. Use these years of child-rearing so that when the child doesn't need you anymore, you've got something you can fall back on.'

What were your obstacles to successful study with the OU?

My workplace wasn't sympathetic. I needed time to go to summer school and that had to be my holiday or my days off. They wouldn't give me time because they said sociology had nothing to do with nursing. But now I'm proving them wrong. The two are closely linked. It's made my life as a nurse so much better. I'm a much broader person on the job than I would have been had I stayed straight in nursing. When I did my degree, my senior manager said to me, 'Why do you want to do that? I've got friends in America who do degrees and then they just die.' I've never forgotten that phrase because she was putting me down. I thought, Well, I'm going to show you. She wasn't helpful. Like at work at night in between cases you could do anything to occupy you so you stay awake. Before I started studying, I read the newspaper or did crossword puzzles, and I had complete and utter peace. But once they saw that I was studying, they would chat to me the whole time. It was a conspiracy, I swear. So in the end I decided never to open a book at work. That's why I studied between 3 and 5 o'clock in the morning. I never mentioned the OU again at work, and they thought I'd given it up.

My self-image was terrible. I could be so scared. I felt I had nothing to offer, and I would put the work down and say, I can't do it, it's rubbish. And then when I'd get it back from the tutor, and he had made such nice comments, it gave me the will to go on. Half-way through, I just did not want to continue. But my husband kept saying, 'Never mind, it might not be as bad as you think it is.' And when I felt that there were just too many sick children, rising prices, working so much harder, there were so many things that made me not want to go on, he would take my books and read the passages for me so that when I am washing up or doing the ironing, I'm listening to his voice.

Tell me about your early education and whether you considered it an obstacle.

Normally you start school at 7 but I was supposed to be quite bright so my mother had me start school at the age of 6. Which meant that if the inspectors came, I was lowered through a window, because I wasn't supposed to be there.

I should have stayed there until I was 15 but my mother took us out to go to secondary school. She took me out at 10. I went to a small secondary school that was run by a brilliant Jamaican teacher, A. S. Clark. I did Junior Cambridge there. We had to do ten subjects. I remember English, geography, history, religious education, hygiene, Latin, maths, Spanish.

Then my father moved me to another school in Montego Bay of the same status. I did the Senior Cambridge exams there. It's the least you're expected to do before you can come out and say you've got something. I didn't want to stay for high school because I wanted to do nursing and I felt it wasn't necessary.

So when I came here for nursing I was very well prepared because we girls from the West Indies had to have advanced education. I came in with Irish girls and English girls who hadn't had any. We had a milkmaid with no education whatsoever. I felt it was unfair that all of us that came from the West Indies had to have so many O-levels, the equivalent of, and yet we were working with girls who had no training at all.

What does the OU mean to you?

Because of the OU, my whole life changed. I used to grumble that my house was too small and there were too many children. But after the OU I could look at a room and see the things that I could do to make it better, whereas before I didn't have that imagination. And the discipline of study. It gives you a fresh eye to look at things.

But primarily it's given me confidence. Things I couldn't do before, I can do now. Like talking to you here, once I would shy away from anything that was a challenge, I would think, I can't do it. My problem-solving ability has got much sharper. I can read and pick up and home in on the important and discard the unimportant quite easily. I don't worry so much anymore about whether I am saying the right thing. I just say what I feel.

Going through all the sociological problems and the humanities, I learned things I had no knowledge of before. Even now, after all these years, I go back to my studies because there were so many things I had not understood that were opened up, for example, statistics. Learning to know what statistics mean when you read something in the paper. I was naive about statistics. Another example is *why* we study history. I always loved history, but was afraid of it because I felt there was so much to learn. But the OU taught me *why* you study history and how you make it a living thing. Before it was dead, just dates, and the OU brought history alive for me.

I never really understood where we fitted into the English world, because you come to England and you are told that your life is owed to England, but the Open University showed us the ways in which the colonies were exploited. And that far from saying, I'm sorry I'm here, thank you very much for all you've given me, I know we helped lay the foundations of this society. We have contributed and are still contributing and that gives you a feeling of belonging. And of saying, I'm here and I'm not begging. I'm prepared to work for what I've got, and you have to respect that.

Only a month ago an Englishman said to me that he didn't agree with the idea that people come here and are given houses. Why weren't they sent back? I really had to remind him that England had lived largely off the colonies. We have always contributed to their well-being and the welfare they now enjoy. So I think they should be mindful of that and not so quick to put us down and to keep us in inferior positions. And they also have a responsibility to the countries they extracted their wealth from.

Tell me some of the ways Jamaican culture has improved traditional UK culture.

When I first came, I found the English very stodgy, stiff upper lip; they didn't mix well, they couldn't dance. They never ate anything but roast beef and Yorkshire pudding. And if food had a smell, they put their noses up. They didn't like our dress because we dressed loudly and wore these things from home. And they didn't like our food because we used onions and garlic and curry. But if you look at the British scene now, I say, they've realized it isn't muck, it's food. And we've taught them to dance, to enjoy themselves, to be more relaxed. I can see very strongly the Caribbean or Jamaican influence. We brought the calypso, we brought the reggae. And on the whole, they dress better now.

I belong to a group called the Mary Seacole Memorial Association. Do you know who Mary Seacole is? Mary Seacole was a Jamaican lady who used to go around the world, and helped during the cholera epidemic during the Crimean War. She worked and paid her way and went to the Crimea. And she helped look after the wounded soldiers because she was what they called a 'sutler', she bought and sold things. And she didn't mind if they were Germans, English, she nursed everybody. Our association feels that she wasn't given the acclaim she deserved because everybody knows about Florence Nightingale who wasn't actually on the battlefield while this woman was dodging in and out, picking up wounded soldiers and tending them. So our society is to make sure everybody knows what she's done.

How about the impacts of the OU on your nursing career?

It has helped me not to despair. This is our third reorganization in nursing. And some of the things in the first reorganization that I could see would happen, nobody else could see. They happened, and I found myself looking at the next stage and saying this is what will happen. And it started happening. And I'm not afraid of accountability; I feel wherever it's taking me, I can go there. But the thing that I'm falling out with is, nursing seems to be forgetting the very reason why we are nurses. I think we are nurses for patients. That's my quarrel with nursing for the moment.

Some of the things that they've changed, I can't see how they benefit patients or look after the weaker members of society. Because they're plunging ahead for those who've got the capital, those who can pay, but they aren't making any provisions for those who cannot.

Community care is a bag of worms. It cannot work in its present form. They haven't made enough provisions, they're not told where they're going to get the money from or how they're going to support the people out in the community. I think it's going to be worse than Victorian times when there was so much poverty behind doors. These are my concerns, especially for the elderly. I mean putting them out into the community as if the community is sitting there all caring, willing to welcome them, it's just amazing. Community is just a buzz word and it's not going to happen. When you're a nurse, you see the uncaring attitudes of relatives and how little time they spend with people in institutions, so you worry, What are they going out to?

Did the OU have anything to do with your becoming a magistrate?

Perhaps. Raising seven children has got to be hard and since they've grown up and they don't need me so much I found that I had a lot of time on my hands. Where I live there are a lot of ethnic minorities, people who don't have opportunities and are not able to express themselves. So we belong to different community groups, like the Commission for Racial Equality and the Hammersmith and Fulham Community Organization. And because of my involvement in the community, the CRE approached me and asked, Did I want to do this? And I said No initially. Then as I got my confidence and they approached me again, I said, 'All right, I'll try.' It's a long interview. Then I waited two years because they go into your background and they have to have the right mix of occupations. They don't want people from just one walk of life.

A lot of blacks who come before the court do not have the support they should have. They have a lawyer but he does not understand, so if their family is not there, nobody is advocating on their behalf. I see a lot of young black people coming in, and when I go out, I say to the parents if your child gets in trouble, the one thing you must never do, no matter how much it upsets you, is allow your child to face the court alone. And a lot of them have no fixed abode. Which is one of the bail conditions. So often they have to go into custody because of fear of absconding.

I would never speak up for a person just because he's black, but if I think that justice is about to be compromised in any way, I do. I hold my ground and try to make them listen. I never go away feeling angry. I might not like the decision, but then, it's two against one. As long as I've made my views known, and if after knowing that, they still decide, then their decision holds. If you are black and you are able to express yourself and you can stick up for yourself, being a magistrate is something you ought to be doing. I argue the same for English people, too, if I feel they are not receiving justice according to what I understand.

What impact has your OU degree had on your performance as a magistrate?

The biggest thing it has done for me is I read and understand, because you have to evaluate what you read. I am able to focus on the salient points easily. My colleagues have noticed that. I pick up on things other people have missed. I write everything down as the people speak. So while the others, who rely on memory, forget things, I've got it written there. And when we are arguing, I call on my notes.

The majority of juries are liberal-minded British people. I've met an awful lot of fair-minded people. But there are some things that they cannot understand, and if there is a miscarriage of justice, it is not their fault. They don't understand the cultural side of it. This is where having black magistrates helps. Because often you get somebody who is black and he might be trying to make a point and he feels frustrated because his education isn't that good. And then he becomes what they call aggressive. To us it is just frustration at not being able to express oneself. So it is very necessary for a black person to be there because we can know whether he is frustrated or just a nasty person.

What is the most important use you make of your OU degree in nursing?

My area was social science and it gave me a greater understanding of people. People tend to come to me for support and advice and I like to think that usually I help them to find their own solution. That is one thing I learned from the OU and dealing with the tutors. They never said to you, 'You're wrong.' They listened to you and everyone had a point of view. Because in nursing you're taught, This is the way it's done. So it's done that way. The OU teaches you that there are other points of view.

Even though I am able to keep up with the field, I am thinking of moving into social services. Nursing has changed, and I'm going to have to lose too much of me to fit into it. And I'm not prepared to do that, I want to be me. So I'm thinking of a career change into social services. I'd like to be involved counselling AIDS victims in some way, from the social work or the counselling side of it.

Have you had any experience with racism in your job as a nurse?

I never, ever failed an interview until I wanted to go beyond a sister and I didn't like the decision that was taken because the interview went very, very well. I came out knowing I had got it because the personnel officer said to me, 'I'll send you the forms.' But the following day she came on the phone and was embarrassed and said, 'I'm sorry, you didn't get it.'

I was very angry and I asked for a full review. My manager said, 'The reason you didn't get the job was because you've done too much night duty.' Now I was going for a night senior manager's post! What better qualification could I have had? She also said the other fellow was more qualified and she reeled off the courses he had done. Okay, may the best man win.

Two blacks and one white male applied, and the white male got the job. I rang the DHSS offices the next day and asked: 'Why was it that if you had done night duty, you could not be given a night senior post?' And they told me there's no such rule. And as time went on, this fellow was no good. He was a terrible manager. Eventually they sacked him because of incompetence. And he hadn't got any of the qualifications that woman said he had.

Subsequently, I acted up in the job. When he left, there was nobody and I was approached to do the job and my friend said, 'Don't do it.' I said, 'No, I will do it, just to show them that I can.' I acted up in the post for a year and I proved myself. Somebody else came in to fill my place. In all fairness to them, they did offer it to me *afterwards*. Because we had a new manager and he said, 'If you want to do it, it's yours,' but I felt that if the previous male manager was the sort of person *they* wanted, then the job's not for me. I'm not in that mould at all.

Why was the OU right for you?

Because I needed to work, obviously, and I could still work and study. And I did it in my own time, when I wanted to, and it wasn't getting up and going off somewhere. Yes, I had to make the tutorials but we had the built-in thing of being able to contact our tutors if we couldn't make a tutorial. It was just so convenient. We didn't have to give up anything; it meant the two things could go together and we didn't suffer the trauma of managing on lower salaries.

I found student support very, very helpful, especially in the early years. We founded a network where, if we were having difficulties, we would ring each other up and say, 'How are you getting on with this?' Because you can ask the tutors but somehow they couldn't be at our level in the first two years with A100 and D101. We needed other students because there were so many of us with different abilities, the tutors probably would have just got fed up with us. So we met at each other's houses and that was great. We'd say, 'Do you mind if we call if we're having difficulties?' Other people would say, 'Well, where do you live?' And we found that we were living in the West 6 area or South-west 6, and that's how it worked, by who was living nearest to you.

How did you balance your OU studies with your family and job responsibilities?

I stayed up late or got up early, whichever fitted. My last son was then at school in the nursery, so I had to take him in the mornings and fetch him back about half past twelve. So while he was gone I left everything and just studied. And when he'd be home in the afternoon, that's when I'd do my homework. My husband was doing the OU at the same time and my children would come to me for something, and I'd say, 'Why don't you ask your Dad because he's had his tea and is free?' And they'd say, 'Oh, no, Dad is studying.' They never, ever saw me as studying. Mum was the person they had to come to.

At the same time it motivated my children. It meant a lot to them. The three younger ones were able to come to our graduation and they'd reached their teenage years where they wanted to go out and work. It really spurred them on. They got back into studying and have done very well for themselves. My son's attitude was, If Mum and Dad can do it, so can I. I had so many friends who after they graduated lost their husbands in some way, and I've got a very good one and I didn't want to lose him, so I said to him, 'Why don't you come with me? At least we could have some things to discuss together, instead of me going off and leaving you behind, because we have exactly the same educational background.' So he agreed and there were days when the tears came, and he would take over the home completely, saying, 'Go on. You can do it.'

Why would you advise women to get an OU degree rather than other kinds of degrees?

That's not an easy one for me to answer because I've never set foot inside a poly. But if you want to do something that allows you to be with your family, and allows you to work, the OU worked for me and it would for other women. The other thing is that it is more difficult to get into a poly because they're looking for grades before you can get there. The OU doesn't do that. You just go in, whatever you are. We had a dustman, we had a builder, we had a man in his eighties. The dustman wanted to do it because he worked in St John's Wood for all these posh people and he wanted to be able to talk with them on their level. We had an early morning cleaner, a lovely lady, who was very ill as a young person and therefore didn't get much schooling and she always wanted to be a teacher. She came to the OU with no background, nothing. And she did eventually get her degree and she became a teacher.

What was the hardest part of study and the easiest?

The hardest part was I was never able to do as much reading as I should have done. I never had the time. The easiest was summer school. It was only a week, but in that time something happened. I felt like I'd been to university, do you know what I mean? You had discussions with people from all walks of life. The tutors allowed you to express yourself, never, ever saying, 'That's rubbish,' even though at times you might say to yourself, 'Oh, that was silly, why did I say that?' They made you think, That's one way of looking at it, and then they'd show you another way, but without putting you down. The units were also easy. The way they are written, by the time you'd get to the end of a unit, they've said it, they've said they said it, and the reinforcement is there; it's painless learning.

To what do you owe your success at the OU?

Determination and self-denial. It was tough. We literally had to say to our friends, 'We can't go out with you anymore.' But they were good friends, because they came back to us so we must have been worth having. But you lose your friends, because you need that time to study. It was study, work, and the family. I became, not quite a slob, but almost. Because you had to prioritize, so I didn't wash the curtains as often as I had. And I learned to cook three or four meals and put them in the freezer instead of doing everything on the day. And I've never gone back. Before I was too particular. I had a wash day and an ironing day and life was just so organized, but I learned you can be less organized and have a better life.

I also involved the family a lot more, because I came from Jamaica where the mother did everything, Dad didn't do anything, except bring the money in. But in doing the OU, Dad had things he could help me do and the children could also be roped in to do things, whereas before I thought children were born to play and have a good time. So the OU helped the children to have discipline as well.

What was most important before and after the OU?

Well, it was always my family and it still is. Although I do many other things, they're the bits of me that I need to keep me afloat, but my centre is still my family. I realize now the part that I must play in fulfilment both for myself and my children, and I see that if I don't keep the family with me, they might become another statistic and I don't want that. Some things are black and white, but I've learned there are grey areas and there are mitigating circumstances and I'm a better mother for having learned it.

———————————————

After interviewing Editha I read, thoroughly enjoyed, and recommend to you Mary Seacole's autobiography, *The Wonderful Adventures of Mrs Seacole in Many Lands* (2nd ed.), edited by Ziggi Alexander and Audry Dewjee (Bristol: Falling Wall Press, 1984).

Chapter 20

University Life's Lack of Fit

Attractive as they are, the FEs [Further Education colleges] have one serious drawback. They are not always geared to the needs of mature students. . . . The mature student is penned in a classroom with a mass of 16- to 18-year-olds – some with a rock-bottom level of motivation. This is where the troubles start. Verbal abuse, ridicule, an uncomfortable classroom climate can quickly develop. The mature student, usually highly motivated, desperately wants to make full use of class time. 'The group' prefers to 'mess about', often at the expense of the mature student. Group dynamics mean the pack rounds on the runt. Too often the mature student is at the receiving end. (Baird, 1993)

Further Education colleges are out of sync with the realities of mature women's lives, and traditional universities tend to be as well. Liz Sperling of Liverpool Polytechnic (1991) has come up with many instances of how university life and women's lives just don't fit. Here are a few examples, with additional evidence that I found from my reading.

Sperling says mature women have to contend with the 'myth of domesticity' held by many men, including university faculty members. They view mature women as unreliable and uncommitted students whose home responsibilities always take precedence over studying. One university in the south of England conveys its belief in the 'myth of domesticity' through a policy of not allowing mother-students to bring their children on site! Mothers cannot take their children even to see what the library is like or show them 'This is where mummy comes when I leave you at the childminder's.' The overall atmosphere at this university is that mother-students shouldn't be there at all (Edwards, 1990).

Another impediment noted by Sperling is the lack of adequate childcare facilities on most university campuses. In her history book's final chapter, 'Echoes into the Late Twentieth Century,' June Purvis (1991) notes that some universities now offer places to mature entrants who pass 'Second Chance' or 'Access' courses. The Catch-22 is that, should they happen to have a nursery, you can bet it is funded by fees and jumble sales. At the same time that there is always adequate and secure funding for sports facilities.

Many mature women, Sperling says, feel intimidated by formal student–staff relationships, lecture teaching methods and male-oriented courses. And because past school experiences made them feel like failures, they are likely to suffer low self-confidence when assessment is by examination, especially when assessment is *only* by examination.

It's hard to believe, but Arlene McLaren (1985) actually found a residential college *for mature women* where instructors use the old teaching technique of 'reading the riot act', that is, routinely telling students that many were going to fail. This unsupportive and divisive tactic only made the women more nervous about failing.

A very good example of lack of fit is the traditional college class timetable which does not take into account women's domestic and family responsibilities. Not surprisingly, even Open University women students give as the biggest reason for not attending tutorials 'conflict with work, home or other non-OU activities' (Millard, 1985).

How do universities convey the notion that they are there basically to train the young for business and industry? This is another problem for mature women students identified by Sperling. Two good ways are a male-dominated faculty and male-dominated administration. Baroness Perry (1992), vice-chancellor of South Bank University, was one of only two women vice-chancellors in over 90 universities and university colleges in the UK in 1992. Less than 4 per cent of professorships in the UK are held by women, so the natural breeding ground for administrators doesn't look all that promising.

What is needed to improve the fit between university life and women's lives?

The following would be a start:

1. Universal entitlement to higher education that could be cashed in at any time in an individual's life and for any type of course.
2. An adequate childcare system.
3. Alternative routes to higher education that are equally prestigious to the straight-through-without-stopping route that young students take.
4. Classes held at times that fit mature students' domestic commitments.

Rosemary Deem and Janet Finch (1986) would add 'single-sex provision' to this list. Why not make available in post-18 education more single-sex colleges and educational packages taught by women? They argue for single-sex education because, 'first, a convincing case has been made by many people that girls' and women's educational performances and experience are improved when they are educated without men'. And second, because non-threatening preparatory courses are needed by re-entering women, particularly by working-class women.

It is also possible for colleges to treat mature students as the assets they are. Which, of course, they want desperately. Supplying a quiet room, an electric kettle and a supply of mugs is the start, says Janet Baird (1992). Once mature students have their safe haven, they should be encouraged to adopt a group identity. Such groups offer self-help, sharing of experiences and study skills sessions. Colleges also can offer counselling sessions directed at mature students' problems and stresses. But finally, colleges can use mature students as a college resource, for example, helping younger students in course revision.

Two women illustrate the lack of fit between women's lives and the operation of traditional universities, Shirleen Stibbe and Gertrude Mtandabari. In Shirleen's case, how else could a mother deliver her kids to school, drive them to violin lessons afterwards, go on to a class on constructing soft toys, *and* go to university – except by doing the OU? Shirleen Stibbe began her first foundation course the day she drove her second son to his first day of school. Twelve courses later she had an honours degree and the satisfaction of having 'been there' for her children – impossible at a conventional university.

As for Gertrude, in 1982 she had an ear operation which left her deaf in one ear. She felt her deafness interfered with being a nurse and began the OU to get ideas of other ways to earn a living. She needed a mode of study which allowed her to hold on to her job and be at home for her two boys. She also needed a way of learning that took deafness into account – as well as the fact that English was her second language. For her first years of OU study, a German-English dictionary was always at Gertrude's side.

Traditional universities ask mature women to fit with them. The OU says, instead, I will fit with you.

Chapter 21

Shirleen Stibbe *From Housewife to Actuary*

As a housewife, your status comes from your husband. For everybody else, you're your husband's wife and your children's mother. But working, I feel like I'm making my own way in the world. It's something that my husband cannot help me with in any degree. At the Open University, he could help me by supporting me or hinder me by demands on my time. But in this, if I make it, then I've made it because I'm me. If I fail, equally, I take full responsibility. I really don't feel master of anything yet. But the feeling that I'm responsible for my own actions is growing.

It was one of those dark, sloshy, blowy late-November afternoons, with delay-causing leaves on the railway lines, when I sat down in the vast foyer of Regent's College with a cat called Charlie and waited for Shirleen Stibbe to appear. She came to our interview exhausted from a training course, where she was preparing for the sixth of ten actuarial exams. 'I certainly didn't need an instructor warning us the whole day long that we'd all certainly fail!' she greeted me.

There are 3,000 actuaries in the UK and they belong to the Institute of Actuaries. One cannot sign documents and act as an actuary unless one is a fellow of the Institute; it was these exams Shirleen was at Regent's College for.

Shirleen is thin, medium height, wears glasses, has short brown hair, and wore a navy sweatshirt and jeans. She was born in South Africa in 1945. Her father was a stockbroker, who died when she was 12. Her mother didn't work until then, when she became an estate agent to support her three children. Shirleen went to an ordinary mixed school and took exams at 17 in English, Afrikaans, French, Hebrew and maths, among other subjects.

She went to Italy for a year after high school, then took a job and also studied part-time at the University of Witwatersrand before getting married in 1967. She and her English husband then moved to the UK, where she became a full-time housewife. She began the OU the day her second child started his first full day at school. She studied from 1978 to 1985, getting a BA with honours. She then earned a PhD in pure mathematics at the University of London, and for two years has worked as a student actuary for a large consultant actuary firm in Epsom. She is the only person of her parental family to get a college degree.

As to why she and Phil came to the UK she said: 'If I couldn't be black and feel I could hold my head up, I wasn't prepared to be white and live in South Africa. It is so overwhelmingly shaming. In those days, 25 years ago, everything that was done to blacks was done in your name. No matter how anti-government you were, or how liberal, or who your friends were, or what you did, everything that was done to blacks was done in your name because you were white. I couldn't live with that.'

What were your reasons for pursuing an OU degree?

I only did it to keep my mind occupied with the boys going off to school. I didn't want a job, because I felt I wanted to be at home, so I just needed something. OU seemed the ideal thing to fill up the odd hour during the day. I started in an uncommitted way, but that first unit of M101 caught me and it was like a drug. The maths we did at school was tedious and dull, and I couldn't ever see the point of it. But M101 suddenly gave me this fantastic structure of interlocking ideas, it just bowled me over.

My family never even thought about mathematics as something people studied. In fact today, people feel mathematics is a very strange thing to have done. When I was at the OU, they'd say, 'What are you studying?' 'Mathematics.' More often than is comfortable to remember, the response was, 'Mathematics????' And then with a certain pride, they would say, 'I was never any good at mathematics!' A very, very strange attitude.

I got this at work the other day, a woman who said, 'I was never any good at mathematics.' I tried to explain to her that if you are a lazy person or don't like complications, then mathematics is just the subject for you. Because what it does is take all those hard, chore-filled things like long division, all the nasty, boring bits, and makes them easy. Instead of dealing with numbers like 4,722.946, if you're a mathematician, you say, 'Well, look, if I can put x for that, then I can fiddle about with the x and life is so much easier.' Then at the end when you've done all the calculations, then you can plug in a number and you do one sum or something. But in school they don't explain how using mathematical methods does away with all the tedium and the complications. I didn't know that either until I started with the OU.

What obstacles or constraints to college study did you have?

I did want to go to university, my mother would have been happy for me to go, but we couldn't afford it. I got a job at the university library, saying, 'Well, if I can't go, I'll be there anyway,' and I studied history of art and psychology just because they sounded interesting to me, through correspondence. Didn't get anywhere with it. The following year I went part-time in my job and did a couple of courses in philosophy and politics and English, but I was a very bad student. That's when I went off to Italy, (a) to get away from South Africa, and (b) do something on my own before I got sucked into this life of being a married woman.

So the only real obstacle was poverty, initially, which is why I didn't go straight off to university full-time. Now I'm glad I didn't because I would have done philosophy, politics and English. I'm no good at them and I'd never have found the wonderful thing that I found. No one ever considered that I might do maths. It was never suggested in school. Women didn't. They didn't mind if you went and studied arts. If you were male, you studied science; if you were female, you studied biology. If you were male, you studied Latin; if you were female, you studied French. At my school there was definitely no thought that women could study any of the science-based subjects.

What does the OU mean to you? How has it been important in your life?

It gave me social confidence. I didn't apply for the PhD programme in the usual way. I just went in and said, 'Look, I want to do this PhD. Who's going to take me on?' It's a status thing to have research students. And analytic number theory, which is very pure, no applications to anything at all, is not at all popular. I had never studied anything having to do with analytic number theory. But this one professor, I was six months older than he was, was happy to have me and I was happy to have him. If I'd stopped doing maths, it would have killed me off.

A more recent example of confidence. Both at work and in actuarial classes, I deliberately ask questions that the other students are afraid to ask. Because I'm not scared any more, I don't care any more, about making an absolute fool of myself. If I don't understand something, and even if I do understand something, I'll ask the question just to clarify. At work I'll go back and say, 'Look, you said this here, explain it. Why have you done this here? What's the background for this?'

When I qualify and represent the firm, I doubt I can be so stroppy. If I am sitting there faced with somebody who is paying this company thousands of pounds for its advice, I can't really be me. I can't sit there and say, 'BS!' I'll say, 'Yes, that's a very interesting point of view. Have you, however, considered . . . ?' I'll have to learn tact and repression and professionalism, straitjacket stuff, so that might be hard.

What impact has your OU degree had on your career?

The mathematics I use a bit, but it's very low-level maths that they need. But the OU discipline is absolutely vital. There's no way I could have got through that first actuarial exam without the discipline because I was doing it totally on my own. I did two on my own. The first one I started studying in January and I wrote in April. The second I wrote in September. The next two I did courses for, but I prefer doing it on my own. I don't like being told 'By this date, you have to have done this much work.' And I don't like being told I'm going to fail all the time. And the OU doesn't badger you, if you don't want to turn in a TMA, you don't have to. My experiences as a student are also useful in my job as an OU tutor, because I do that too. I've been doing it for three years. I take two or three day schools a year, I mark people's assignments, I talk to them for hours on the telephone, and a week ago I spent four glorious days in Milton Keynes working 14 hours a day marking examinations. I can't tell you what it was like to spend four days without an actuarial thought in my head with people that I like, who are mathematicians and who talk about mathematics and not economics or mortality.

Did the OU teach you to see your work differently, to perhaps wish to transform your profession?

Yes, yes, yes, indeed I do. In my current situation, all I can do is carp. But when I've qualified, I can start carping in the right directions. Now, I would be totally ignored if I wrote a letter to the Institute of Actuaries and said, 'This profession needs this and this and this.'

Think about what's happened to accountants. They're now perceived as being incompetent, perceived as being against the public interest in that they give a clean bill of health to a company which then goes bust two weeks later. The actuarial profession is going in the same direction. We give advice to employers, but we don't take into account that actual pensioners and people buying insurance also need protection. And that they need *our* protection. The profession serves the people who pay and the people who pay are the employers. Now just as in a legal case, the employers have their actuary and the trustees their actuary, but the pensioners don't have an actuary advising them.

What's the most important use you make of your OU degree?

The reason I wanted to be a tutor was because when I finished my OU degree, and I went into the outside world, I felt absolutely rejected by my mother, as it were. The thought of spending the rest of my life not associated any more with the OU was appalling. So I did my very best to crawl back into it in some way. They had this course, Mathematics in Computing, which nobody wanted to teach, so they called me in.

I put a lot of chat on the assignments themselves if I disagree with something. And I put lots of comments on the tests. And the PT3 forms are enormously important to students because you're giving them an overall comment on their script. They can't tell the tone of your voice, so you don't joke. And you must use the sandwich principle. That means you have to start out by saying something encouraging, then you can put your criticisms down, but you have to end up on a high note as well. Nice, nasty, nice.

You can't say, 'If you had spent a bit longer on this TMA, you would have done better.' Because the student might have spent hours and hours and hours. You've got to bear in mind that somebody might be writing a TMA with her husband screaming at her and her child pulling the kettle down. People are working under a huge range of different circumstances, so you've got to be very careful with criticism. Imagine somebody going through a divorce and you make a comment like, 'You really must concentrate more!' At a conventional university there is a certain authority a lecturer has over the students, but we don't have that at the OU. I can't moan and groan at them. All I can do is say, 'I know this unit's a bit difficult to interpret' and make tentative suggestions.

Were there any liberal arts transfers from your OU degree to your job?

It gave me confidence in my social skills. We're not a terribly social family. We're very busy with our own personal pursuits and don't have a huge circle of friends. Summer schools, where you have to work intensively with a partner on a project, a partner who was a total stranger to start with, helped me. I really hit it off with my science foundation partner. We had such fun turning purple substances yellow and watching them turn back to purple, and classifying rocks and doing physics experiments.

But still, socially, I sometimes put my foot in it in the worst way. I've got this theory – it's not a real theory – about sociology. It is that most OU students studying sociology are in prison or out on parole. So my first day at the quantum theory summer school I went into the canteen and sat down next to this other student, and the first question you ask is, 'What are you studying?' And he said, 'Sociology.' And I said, 'Oh, really! What were you inside for?' And he was aghast. 'How did you know? Have they been talking about me?' He'd just come out of prison. He'd been in for drug dealing. Oh, I wanted to crawl away. I was only trying to get the conversation going.

Why was the OU right for you?

Because the maths faculty was so supportive. You have at the end of the telephone a person you can phone up and say, 'Help!' in the middle of the night. You can't do that at conventional universities. I'm astounded at how little support students get at conventional universities. They're told to go to the lectures and get on with it, but at the OU they are there to help you and they will you to get through the exams. At a conventional university they don't care. All the lecturers are interested in is their research. You can't blame them because that's how they get their promotions.

When I was at Royal Holloway I marked assignments for various classes. And the assignments showed me what the students didn't understand and needed help with. But the lecturers had no idea the students weren't getting the material. At the end of the year, 41 per cent failed and the faculty threw up their hands in horror, 'How could this happen?'

How did you balance your OU studies with your family responsibilities?

I stopped doing housework. The boys were sometimes ashamed of me because their mother was not the same as other people's mothers. They would have liked to have had a good housewife with a clean house, busy baking bread. They couldn't bring friends home unexpectedly because they knew the house would be a total wreck. This became clear when we became concerned with Darian's delayed walking. He was a reasonably adequate child, why wasn't he walking? But one day we were having guests, so I tidied up and we were sitting about playing music and he got up and danced. He hadn't walked because the floor was so littered, he had no place to put his feet, so he just crawled about in the mess. Now here he was, dancing to Mozart on this clean floor.

My family was vital to my OU success. My husband pushed me through it. I'd get despondent, I can't get this CMA done, I can't pass this exam. 'Come on', he'd say, 'you said the same thing last year. You said the same thing the year before.' I couldn't have stuck it out to such a committed degree without him there, egging me on.

The OU certainly influenced the boys. There was never any question they would get a degree and it's pushing them on to do higher degrees as well. It's very hard when you're 18 and can't dismiss your parents as obsolete. Kids feel they have to do better than their parents. If I'd got my PhD twenty years ago, it would be easier for them to say, 'Well, *today* it would be harder.' The fact that it's recent represents a challenge. Darian is in his second year of physics at Oxford, and Arran, who got a first degree in computer science from York University, is getting a MSc in computational linguistics at Edinburgh.

Why would you advise women today to get an OU degree versus other options?

Because many mature women go to college the first year thinking, I can do nothing. But if they have a good foundations course tutor–counsellor, they get rid of that sense of failure in the first year. When they pass their first year, then they know they can do anything. That first year is absolutely vital, and the OU is brilliant in their foundation courses. The build-up of confidence is marvellous in that first year if you've got the right teacher–counsellor.

What was the easiest part of OU study?

I found summer school easy and also fascinating. Most students behave like ordinary people but the exceptions are always there too. There's the 42-year-old tart who is studying sociology and you can see a beacon from her eyes to the first tutor whom she fancies and then you can watch her grab him and nab him and not let the poor guy go until the end of the week. Then there's the type who always gets her handbag stolen or falls over a chair and hurts her ankle, a little girl who needs help. There's also the organizer. He will write to the OU and say he's sorry but he's going to arrive late, could they please keep a room for him? And then he will arrive the day before, due to circumstances, and announce, 'I'm the special case.' He will then pick the best room in the place because he's made himself special. And he'll have his bevy of women who do things for him, like wake him up in the mornings.

There's the female tutor who feels out of her depth with all the male tutors and she'll try to be swinging and with it at the disco. But male students aren't interested in female tutors, they're interested in female students. And female students aren't interested in male students, they're interested in male staff. They are like teenagers, their chains broken, no longer Mrs M from number 10 who has three pints on a Thursday.

How good a degree do you think the OU degree is?

I don't think, academically, an OU degree has any particular advantage. But it does say more about you as a person than a conventional degree. And what an employer should draw from the fact of your OU degree is that you are able to work on your own, that you are able to commit yourself to a project and complete it, that you have self-discipline, and that you stick to things. Whether they draw this conclusion or not is another matter. I have found a lot of ignorance about the OU. Some people who should know better think that it is easy. I was told by a lecturer at Royal Holloway, 'Well, Shirleen, you've done as well as you possibly could have done at the Open University, but you know, the assignments and exams of the OU are very benign. I'm not sure that you would actually be able to go that step further for a PhD.'

To what do you attribute your success with the OU?

Hard work. I worked very hard on the foundation course because I didn't know anything, but the materials got me through. After that, I had no ambitions to come up with a great mathematical theory, but I did try. I did spend hour after hour trying to prove different things, famous maths problems, like Fermat's last theorem – there's a similar one in analytic number theory, which everyone knows is true but it's never actually been proved – and I spent hours and weeks and months trying to find a bit of proof of these things and never got anywhere. A good jobbing mathematician is what I became, but not an inspirational mathematician.

Tell me about your new career and your plans. To start with, what was it like looking for work with two mathematics degrees but no experience?

I had to sit down and think who would actually want me. I knew there was a local branch of an actuarial consultancy in Epsom, where I live, so I phoned up the personnel office and I said, 'Hello, my name is Shirleen Stibbe and I am the answer to the demographic timebomb.' And he said, 'Hello?' So I began again in a more sombre tone. I told him my situation, I said, 'I've got this PhD degree,' and asked, 'Are you interested in employing me in any form?' And he said, 'I'll send you an application.'

I filled in the form, not thinking at all about actuaries or what they do. I listed what I'd done, degrees and everything, and then he wrote and said two of the partners were interested. So I went along for an interview, still not knowing anything about actuaries. And we had a long chat and they said, 'Well, we are in need of technical staff.' And I said, 'Ahhh, does that mean non-actuarial?' 'Yes,' they said, 'non-actuarial.' I said, 'Ah, what about actuarial staff?' 'No, no,' they said, 'we recruit actuarial staff from graduates in September every year. And the only post that we have is for technical staff. But you can have a very good career in technical staff.' 'Great,' I said, 'however, if I come and work for you as technical staff, will you support me if I take the actuarial exams on my own?' 'Yes, yes, certainly my dear,' pat on the head, thinking the old bag'll never make it.

And later I said, 'I've passed, you see, so how about taking me on as actuarial staff?' 'Umm, umm, we'll think about it,' they said. Being actuaries, of course, they are very cautious people. So I plunged into the second course. Then suddenly they wrote me a letter and said we've decided to make you actuarial staff and immediately my salary went up £5,000, which has increased with each exam I've passed.

These exams represent a real challenge. I find them very much harder than OU exams, even harder than doing a PhD, mainly because they are *not* stimulating intellectually. Economics and mortality, it's tedious stuff. I find it very hard to sit down and do it. With my OU courses, having to go and fetch the children from school became a real grind if I wanted to carry on.

But I'm pathetically grateful to the firm for taking me on at age 44. In general, people won't take on 50-year-olds because (a) you may be older than these young managers, and (b) you may be more experienced. They don't want to take on people who are going to show them up. And they have a fear that you're *not* going to be manipulated.

What was most important in your life before the OU and most important now?
It used to be my husband and family and still is, but now *I* also come first. Before the OU, husband and family were much more important than my own requirements. Feminism hadn't reached South Africa when I was growing up. I don't know if feminism has reached South Africa yet. Women didn't have their own careers, they all had servants. The work ethic, the self-esteem ethic, the my-own-value ethic, hadn't filtered through in my childhood and it wasn't something I thought about at all. But I got involved with the OU and I suddenly discovered that perhaps there is a real person in here.

As we were saying goodbye, I said that surely actuaries weren't as dedicated to their jobs as she'd implied. So she told me this joke. Three men are discussing their jobs, a lawyer, an accountant and an actuary. The lawyer says he has a great life, he is well paid, has an excellent wife, bit of a nag, but he has a fabulous mistress. 'And with the sort of job I have, all I do is tell my wife I've got to work late and off I go to my mistress.' The accountant said, 'Oh, my life is also wonderful, only my mistress is a bit demanding, but because of my job, I just tell my mistress that I've got to work late, and then spend more time with my wife.' And the actuary says, 'Ah, no, no, no, you two. I have a much better life. I tell my wife I'm with my mistress and I tell my mistress I'm with my wife, and I get to work late!'

Chapter 22

Gertrude Mtandabari

From Nurse to Daycare Co-ordinator

> **P**eople think I'm a bit odd because for the last ten years I've been doing all these courses. And I ask myself sometimes, Why am I doing this with my life? My aim now is to finish a counselling diploma, but when I do, I'll be 56 and should be thinking about retirement. But I was a late starter in everything. I married late. My education was late. My realization of what my needs were was late. There was a time when I didn't question anything, I just got along with my life and brought up my children. But as I got older, I wanted more.

On my first visit to Gertrude's house in 1991, I rode the Underground out to Canons Park in bright November sunshine. It was a Saturday morning. I handed up two milk bottles when she answered the door. When a woman's surname is Mtandabari, you aren't expecting a plump, blue-eyed, blonde-haired, pale-skinned woman with an Austrian accent. It was Gertrude's husband, who died of a heart attack four years ago, who was from Zimbabwe.

Gertrude was born in 1938 in a little village outside Linz. She left school at 14, became a qualified sick children's nurse, and worked in Austria until she came to England in 1968. She had met her future husband on a train bound for Austria in 1965. After years of correspondence, they married and Gertrude started her UK nursing career as an auxiliary at the sick children's hospital in Hackney. Her nursing registration came through, she had her first child in 1969, and went to work part-time in Edgware Hospital. She completed a mental handicap nursing course in 1974, and started the OU in 1983 shortly after a failed operation which left her deaf in one ear. She got her BA in 1989. She has two sons, aged 22 and 19.

What were your reasons for pursuing an OU degree?

Whenever I saw OU broadcasts on TV, I always wanted, somehow, to get into it. But I had a full-time job, I had children, I thought I wouldn't have the time. The learning side of it was for me fascinating. But then I had an operation on my ear which left me deaf. I felt I wasn't a complete person anymore. There was something missing, something that would affect my professional service. I found it difficult communicating everywhere at first. With no hearing aid I didn't have enough hearing to understand everything. With an aid I couldn't hear in crowds because of background noise.

I didn't know what I should do instead of nursing, but I thought through the OU courses, I would come to some ideas in the end. I have always wanted to do counselling. But I found the psychology courses too theoretical.

What obstacles did you overcome to do the OU, apart from your hearing loss?
My husband was not in favour of me doing the OU. He would help me with the housework, but he would do this anyway whether I was studying or not. He was not keen for me to study. Maybe he was a bit afraid. What am I going to do next? His education was very poor, very basic. He worked first as a chef and then a cab driver.

My social life also suffered, but I never did go out a lot. It was difficult to have a full-time job and then go home and read your books. TV had to be cut back and there was no time for reading magazines.

Then I also had a language problem. At first I thought I couldn't do it without proper English, looking up the meaning of every other word in a dictionary. It was very hard work. My English was never that good. So writing all those assignments, it was a nightmare for me.

I chose courses which didn't have summer schools that would take me away from my family and because I found it difficult to make contact with other people there. They only do the special hearing groups with that foundation course. I miss things, especially in big groups. I can hear the tutor but if we sit behind one another, I can't hear other people.

Tell me about your early schooling.
My primary school was mixed, boys and girls, ages 7 to 10, and there were between 30 and 40 in a room with a teacher, children of three different ages all in one room. A lot of us were put back because of the war.

Then I was in another village for two years where we lived with my mother's parents, because my father was a prisoner of war in Russia. Eventually we moved to a town called Wels, where we had a pub. I had tremendous difficulties with the change of country, people, everything. I didn't get to know my father until he came home from the war, because I was born in 1938 and the beginning of '39 my father had to go to war. And he didn't come home until '47. Our house was demolished by bombs and we lived with our grandparents while my mother put everything back together.

So I went to two very basic schools. Then because my parents had a pub and wanted me to work there, I left school at 14. They wanted me to do something in catering so they sent me away to a boarding school for eight weeks a year for three years. I was very shy, I'm still quite shy. My parents never had any great expectations of me, they simply expected me to work in the family business. They thought catering school would do me good, but the boys did all the cooking and the girls did all of the cleaning. I only finished it because my parents wanted me to.

I wanted to work with children. So I had an interview in Vienna to work with deprived children but they didn't find me suitable, probably I was so shy. So I studied sick children nursing in Linz and qualified after three years. I stayed there and worked and one day I went on holiday and met my husband which led to my coming to England.

What does the OU mean to you?
If I had stayed in Austria, I wouldn't have done any studying at all. I would be quite happy looking after a husband and children because that's what Austrian women lived for. But

having had opportunities here, to which the OU contributed a lot, yes, my expectations have changed and my views have, too. I did social science subjects. I never knew anything about politics, and I was always a very conservative person, that's how I was brought up, and always voted Conservative, and with the OU I learned to question everything. I was very confused at first because the issues which came up in my social science courses made me think.

I support the Labour party now because their whole history supports welfare more than the Conservative party. This trust business has affected our centre badly. Our unit has applied for trust status. And we can see it already now, when people leave, they're not being replaced. Because they have a certain budget and they have to provide essential services for the money they've been given. And in our small unit, domestic service, which has always been done by the health service, has now gone private. People have been made redundant and no extra help has been employed, so those who are still employed are doing the jobs of the people made redundant. And on the nursing side, people who have left have not been replaced. So now we're back to basics, where you provide a service to survive, feeding, dressing, and basic hygiene. My daycare was an additional service, and I still provide it, but for a smaller number of people.

The OU has helped me personally because if I do find another shy person, I may make the first contact. Now I fight against my shyness. A lot of people are shy like me, so why not open up a bit more? If you think about my whole lifestyle, I have had this need to care for people because I feel safe in it. I could never go out in the business world. You have to be ruthless in the world of business, and I can't see myself doing that.

Did the OU change you in any other important ways?

The OU changed me to a more generous person, a less narrow-minded person. There was a tremendous generosity about my husband. He fascinated me, he was a different person from everybody else I knew. To give you an idea of how I used to be, we had already arranged our registration to get married on Christmas Eve, and we had an argument over religion, quite a silly thing, and as a result, he cancelled the arrangements for the registration. We still got married, two weeks later. But it would have been on Christmas Eve instead of the 9th of January. Why did we argue? I was very religious at that time, and my husband was a Catholic, but he didn't have a baptism certificate, so no Catholic church would marry us.

I felt that I couldn't get married without him being a Catholic, or without him having the commitment, or whatever. So religion was a big problem for a start. But later on, it wasn't, because I changed. One of my OU courses was on religion. Now I see myself as a Christian, not a Catholic. I don't have to go to a Catholic church. My husband was a better person than me, and his religion had nothing to do with it. He was sceptical about religion and the only time he would come with me to church was Christmas Eve to Midnight Mass. He did it just because it meant so much to me.

Tell me about the impact of your OU degree on your career.

I was working shifts as a sister of the ward at a residential treatment centre for the handicapped. I have been there since 1980. But there has always been a need for more than mere physical care, just feeding and dressing. There is a need for psychological care as well.

I had asked to do a counselling course through work. Because it would have involved working hours, I was not allowed to do it. Also it was not considered necessary in nursing. They thought I had acquired these skills, as it were, over the years. So I was quite unhappy about that. But finally I had a new boss who was implementing changes and he asked if I would like this job. I would be the first daycare co-ordinator. He knew I wanted to change, and he knew I was enthusiastic about the changes he was implementing. He wanted to give people living in settings like this more opportunities.

I didn't know how to start, what hours I should work. I was completely on my own. I started doing this in 1988, the year before I finished my OU degree. I was very excited but I had no experience and I didn't get much support from the rest of the staff. Eventually we employed another two people to help me to expand the daycare programme. Whatever I wanted to do, my boss has been behind me.

Our unit became two units and we added short-term care for people coming from home where their mothers needed a break. One big unit also was not compatible with having some people with challenging behaviour and other people who are very dependent.

The course which helped me the most was The Handicapped Person and the Community. The first thing I implemented was goal planning, which I learned through the OU: ways of identifying needs of individuals and working on the strengths of individuals. Short-term goals, long-term goals, and I used these plans. I was promoted eventually because of my goal planning. I was graded a sister's grade and you can appeal, which I did because I don't consider myself a nurse anymore, I'm a nurse specialist. So I got a promotion, a new title, and one or two thousand pounds a year more.

Why was the OU right for you?
I prefer studying at home but I also went to the OU because they support disabled people. If you look into any other university, they don't ask if you can cope or not, whereas the OU discriminates positively. They find out what sort of problem you've got and then see how they can help you. For example, you were given extra time on examinations because of your disability. I never found this anywhere else. They also supplied me with a hearing aid. I was having difficulties when we had tutorials of 10 or 15 people in one very big room. I had problems picking up the voices and understanding. Their loop system helps you by cutting out the background noise. Also the tutors were informed that I was disabled and would personally ask me what my requirements were. They had respect for whatever I needed and tried to supply it.

At my first summer school in Brighton I wasn't happy. Because of my hearing problem, I isolated myself from the rest. But at the second one, the arts foundation, they had a special summer school at Keele for hearing-impaired people and it was fantastic. We had all kinds of aids because people need different aids. Some had no hearing at all. The OU had special equipment for us, some needed computers to read with, and we had somebody who signed. Working together in that small group was lovely. I'm still in contact with one lady I met on that course. She's in her late sixties and doing honours. We all had something in common, the disability, not being able to cope under normal circumstances, and it made us jell.

Why would you advise a friend to do OU rather than a regular college?

Studying at home suited me. I can study whenever I want to at home, choose my time. The way it's organized suited me, they don't ask you for any qualifications, they don't give you a test. And the way the books are structured, you begin slowly. They don't assume anything. Everything is explained so thoroughly, it doesn't matter what background you have. I come from a different country, had an Austrian education, and I thought I might not be able to follow it because of my lack of vocabulary. I translated every word I didn't understand at first, but in the end you get the feel of it and you understand the words as you go along. I didn't need a dictionary after a year. New words I didn't understand appeared again and again and I got the meaning as I went along. Meeting once a week, discussing the books was so supportive. A friend of mine was doing a distance-learning course with some other college and she gave up because there was no support.

What quality in you was responsible for your success with the OU?

I had never thought of myself as being able to pass all those exams because I've never been academically bright. So it was just through perseverance and wanting to go through it that I've made it, really. Whatever I start I want to finish.

Although it was very hard having to work full-time and my husband died as well during that time, I had something to work for. Even after my husband died I wanted to carry on. I didn't suffer from any severe depression because I had this aim, I wanted to finish the OU. I do feel now that if I can do the OU, anybody else can do it. If you put your mind to it and work hard, you can do it, you don't have to be very, very bright academically.

My husband didn't realize how much time it would involve, me studying and carrying on with a full-time job. He thought something would have to give. Either the children would get less of me or the housework would be neglected. One time I thought I'd retire from work because of the way he felt. But I would not give up the OU. I was determined to make it to the end.

What are your career plans?

I'm doing a skilled help counselling course with the Harrow Polytechnic, an 18-week course. Also I have applied for the diploma in counselling, and that would be another two years through Harrow. The OU doesn't have any counselling courses. My employer supplied 100 per cent for a management course I just finished and will pay 50 per cent of the skilled help course.

Yes, I failed my most recent OU course, Management and Mental Health, a half-credit course. I was very disappointed at first. There were several reasons why I didn't pass. One reason was we didn't have an experienced tutor, it was his first year, and he obviously has never done anything like this because he works for the health service. He gave us a lot of extra material which it wasn't possible to get to, and we never discussed the books from the OU. I thought I would be perfectly all right because I was used to OU studies. I was confident I'd get through it. Well, I didn't. The course had a very high percentage of failure. We were fifteen in the course and five of us failed and one was a consultant.

But another reason I failed was my heart wasn't there any more, because I had already started my counselling course towards the end of that course.

As far as my future goes, I don't take too many risks. At the moment, I would like to stay where I am and do mental handicapped counselling. I hope I'll get support from my boss for me doing it. Even though mentally handicapped persons can't express themselves as well as normal persons, they have feelings and emotions and because they can't express their thoughts verbally, their need for counselling might even be greater. And they can express themselves in body language and behaviour.

I'm already putting this course to practice at work. For example, one young man in his late twenties is autistic. He can't express himself verbally. What he does is, he bangs doors, bangs against the windows, pushes other people aside, and throws things. In the past, staff often shouted at him. So I'm struggling with staff, trying to make them understand that he can't say what frustrates him, and to ignore the bad bits of his behaviour and pay attention to the good bits. I have individual sessions with him at least once a week, one hour in a darkened room with dim lights and mats on the floor and the walls. We go in and I play very soft, relaxing music. For a start he is very restless. There's a mirror in there. He looks at himself and bangs very hard. This has improved already. I don't stop him from banging, because there's nothing he can damage and he does not attack me, always things.

Eventually he will sit down, and curl up and relax. There are a few things I concentrate on such as eye contact. He doesn't look at you. This has improved. Then I go over with him the positive things I've found during the day, but also some of the negative things, I go over them, just talk about them. You always know when he's happy and unhappy. He can make a lot of happy noises. I've got a tape which I play with his favourite tunes. I start the session with a tune which is always the same and finish with the same tune, so that it marks his time to do what he likes.

When I play his favourites, he hums along. Then I'll play a few new tunes and he just curls up and listens. I feel he gets a lot out of it, but his aggressive behaviour outside is the same because the staff continue to treat him as a bad boy and he resents people shouting, 'Don't do that!' So we are talking a lot now, how the staff have to change so that he can change.

What was most important in your life before the OU and after?
My family, my husband and boys, have always been the most important thing. My husband was the type of man who wanted to please everybody. He was very considerate. He didn't want to cause any trouble at all. He always thought about what other people might be thinking about him. He didn't want to live in an area where there were a lot of black people, because he would then be judged as one of them. Even with his own sons, he didn't want them to have friends from the West Indies because he identified them with crime and unemployment. He didn't want my sons' friends in the house because he thought they would influence the boys badly. So I was always the one who wanted everybody to come in, it didn't matter who it was.

The boys had to do what he wanted them to do, which was get a good education, because he was deprived of it, and they had to become something more than he was, because he didn't achieve for lack of education. He was strict and I was the one who always gave in and tried to smooth things out.

Earlier we were talking about obstacles to your succeeding at the OU. It sounds as though being married to a black man in Britain was an obstacle?

Yes, it was an obstacle. I felt racism through my children a lot. Like I've told you, my husband felt he had to make up for things which other black people might have done wrong. He was very helpful with neighbours, very considerate, where I just wanted to live my life. For example, when we would come home late in the evening, he would switch off the engine because he didn't want to wake up the neighbours. He wanted to be seen as different from other black people and in a way it was discrimination against his own people.

My elder son had a lot of problems at school but he would never want us to go to school and find out about it. He felt he would be bullied more for not being able to stand up for himself. Even now he'll say, 'You have no idea how much I hated that school.' It was an old Catholic boys' school. He got very aggressive and was expelled. At the time we thought he was a bad boy. But years later he told me people teased him and he wouldn't have it, so he started fighting. He's very bright but he didn't want to go further than that. He finished secondary school and had one or two O-levels, one was in art. He completed a bricklaying course, some courses in drawing, and he went into a lot of sports. He won a boxing competition. He scared me because all his aggression came out. He's given up boxing, but he still does a lot of physical sports like football. It took him a long time to find out what he wanted to do. Now he's self-employed and has done quite well. He trained in jewellery-making and finds it very satisfying that he can work for himself.

Even my younger son, who was doing very well at school, was put back in English from the top group to a lower level, and I questioned it because one of my son's friends had a lower mark in his test and he was allowed to stay in the top group. Eventually my son went back up to the top group because I complained. After that, my husband arranged for him to have private lessons so that he would stay on top. So he did from then on, really stay on top. He finished three A-levels – chemistry, biology and mathematics – and he's studying medicine now at University of London medical school.

How do you relate to your sons now? What kinds of problems do grown children have?

My problems with them are my problems. I make them my problems. I'm not studying now. If I could be studying, my time would be taken up. I'd have a substitute for them.

But in the meantime it's a convenience having a mother who washes your clothes and feeds you and they can do what they want. But my two sons react completely different. My elder son said recently, 'You know, you're a very good mother. Most mothers wouldn't do the cooking and the washing for their grown sons.' And I thought, Well, there must be a need in me to do it. He doesn't say, 'I want this and I want that.' It's me. It's my need to mother him.

My other son only comes home at weekends. And he usually comes home with a girlfriend, in spite of my Catholic upbringing. I've got used to that. I say, 'You don't have to ask anymore. It's your life, you're old enough.'

He never tells me when he's coming because he says, 'I don't want to tell you, otherwise you start cooking for me.' Last week he came with his friend at 10 o'clock and I felt I had to fix something. And he said, 'No, Mum, we are going to get a pizza.' And I said, 'Why don't you want a proper meal?' And he got very angry with me and said, 'I don't want you to cook anything. Why do you always do this?'

In the end I gave in. He's right. Why should I be doing it? Why don't I start another course?

Chapter 23

The Homemaker Role

Dons at Cambridge University are investigating the underachievement of women. Although 4 out of 10 undergraduates are female, in some subjects they bag less than 10 per cent of first-class degrees. . . . Having sifted through all the permutations I have sadly come to the conclusion that women's failure to win first-class degrees is just another symptom of our cock-eyed society. From such an early age we are encouraged not to achieve excellence, but to get along until it is time to marry and have babies. Motherhood is our only real metier, and that is where we should excel, in providing a safe, nourishing ambience for our young, so our little boys may grow to excel and our little girls may grow to be just like mummy. (Lonsdale, 1993)

The last, but by no means least, obstacle to women's education is our socialization to be wives and mothers, caregivers and homemakers. This socialization goes way beyond male-biased school readers, teachers paying more attention to boys and educational policies drawn up by male politicians. Children confront this socialization through toys, books, advertisements, clothes, television, films, peer culture – you name it. It starts with the strongest purveyors of all, mothers and fathers.

Hundreds of erudite books have been written about sex-role socialization. Here I give it the same space as the other nine obstacles, but that doesn't mean it is not probably the biggest single obstacle to women's educational achievement.

The seriousness of sex-role socialization for motherhood was underscored in Joan Wheeler-Bennett's (1977) *Women at the Top*. She studied 65 highly qualified women who were successfully balancing careers and families. Yet, she identified as the Number 1 obstacle to their careers the wife–mother role. It took enormous determination, organization and hard work for them to take care of all the people in their lives – children, husbands, domestics, dependants, invalids – and to overcome, because of these very same people, interrupted or late-starting careers. If being a wife–mother was a problem for these talented, affluent women, how much more of a problem is it for 'the average woman'?

How do girls and young women get socialized to be homemakers?

Birthday cards portray girls as decorative and domestic, boys as active and adventurous. Toy catalogues feature a Little Girls' Cleaning Trolley complete with vacuum cleaner, apron and cap, dustpan and brush. Local newspapers show pictures of junior beauty queens. Magazine ads picture girls and mothers shopping together. In the comics female characters are shown most as shoppers, mums and housewives (Women's Monitoring Network, 1987).

Joyce Nicholson (1980, p.17) paints the following sorry picture of the outcome of early conditioning:

> Unfortunately this conditioning imposed on girls in pre-school and early school life not only greatly colours the view they have of themselves and their future role in life but it also influences their attitude towards their education and their achievement in education, and this is a much more serious matter. A woman can, in later life, look back on the conditioning to which she was subjected, and she can overcome it to some extent, but if it has resulted in her not making the full use of her educational opportunities, she usually finds herself in a position where she cannot alter her situation.

In 1980 the Women's Media Action Group started to keep tabs on how women are portrayed in newspapers and magazines and on television and radio. Their most recent summary said that the media continue to perpetuate the myth that domesticity is the sphere of greatest relevance to women.

> The media also collude with the myth that women and domesticity are linked *by nature* – this is their *natural* role. This of course provides a rationale for continuing to expect women to do most of the household work, and enabling men to escape its confines. There is virtually no recognition in any part of the media that men do (or could, or should) play a role in the domestic sphere. (Davies, Dickey and Stratford, 1987, p.168)

Things domestic, including child-rearing, are, at the same time, devalued and seen as unimportant and incidental because they are just part of women's nature.

What happens in maturity to socialize women to the predominant role of homemaker?

One thing is – we keep on reading women's magazines! Their editors want us to believe that everyday life, organized around the family, is worth living every day, regardless of the trials sent to test us. Features revolve around marital problems but present these problems as always overcomeable; problems just reinforce the marriage bond! We are given advice on beauty and fashion, cookery and do-it-yourself home projects, all portrayed as pleasure and leisure, not hard work. Short stories concentrate on getting a man, the difficulties in any marriage when children are young, and life when children leave home. Even horoscopes are saturated with relationships to boyfriends and close relatives.

No wonder a 1992 study of who does what household chores concluded that the gap between attitudes and practice *has widened over the years*. 'Sex equality' reported that today washing and ironing are done mainly by women (84%), shared equally by 12%, and done mainly by 3% of men. Evening meals are prepared mainly by women (70%), shared equally by 20%, and done mainly by 9% of men. But equally dismaying is the fact that people's ideals are so far off their behaviour. Washing up after the evening meal *should* be shared equally say 75% of people, but only 37% actually share the task. Cleaning *should* be shared equally say 60%, but only 27% share it. This particular survey didn't pose the question, 'And who should be at home for the children,' but what would your guess be?

Probably 75% would say it *should* be shared equally, but again, the reality is that women do it 75% of the time.

———————————

I chose two women to illustrate women's socialization to be a wife and homemaker, Janaki Mahendran and Val Burke. When Janaki began the OU in 1984 she had two small children and while doing her degree had another baby. She also takes care of her mother-in-law, who lives with them, and her parents, who live in the next street. Janaki's attempts to get a medical degree in her birthplace, Sri Lanka, were thwarted primarily because of her difficulties with the English language. What better way to deal with her language problem than the OU and also have the flexibility to take care of her extended family.

Val Burke of Sheffield did the OU so that she could be at home when her daughters' school day was finished. Her interests today, apart from her job, are strictly centred in her home. I found her bookshelves loaded with popular romantic novels, a new knitting machine being set up in the front room, and Val looking forward to working in her big back garden the next summer. Indeed, one of the best sides to Val's new career as a computer programmer is her salary, which goes towards making family life for them all much more comfortable.

Chapter 24

Janaki
Mahendran

From Volunteer to Conflict and Change Educator

When I went to the OU, I met many interesting people and had the opportunity to learn about the way they talk, the way they dress, the way they think. And my job now is entirely different from my background in the sciences. I had no social work training but the OU gave me what I needed for my job. Coincidentally, the OU is starting a new course called Managing Volunteer Organizations and for that our project was selected, and they came and filmed some of my workshops with the children for that course.

Janaki Mahendran lives in Ilford, where many of the street names end in 'Gardens'. We did the first interview in her front room, looking out at people's little front gardens, and the second interview in colourful East Ham, at Christopher House where she works for a registered charity, the Newham Conflict and Change Project.

Janaki is a tiny, slight woman with light-brown skin and long, shiny, straight black hair in a braid. She is full of energy and smiles readily. While I watched the sun set through her lacy curtains, she fixed us tea and put a box of biscuits on the coffee table. I met her husband, who is a general practitioner, as he left on an errand, and two of her three children, who did their homework very quickly, and then gradually made their way down the stairs playing a different game on each step.

Briefly, Janaki's husband brought her and the two older children to England in 1983 on holiday . While they were here, fighting broke out in their homeland, Sri Lanka, and it was too dangerous for them to return. Because her husband's occupation is 'useful', the UK government made no fuss about their being allowed to stay. So her husband found a position and Janaki started the OU. Her previous education in Sri Lanka had been A-levels followed by two years of teacher training in the sciences. Today Janaki's mother-in-law lives with them and her parents are just a street away.

They are all now naturalized citizens and have British passports because, although they didn't want to change their old passports, if you travel with a Sri Lankan passport, Janaki says, people think you are trouble.

What were your reasons for doing an OU degree?
I found out about the OU through their television programmes, seeing the normal advertisements. I didn't know anything about the OU. They ended up the programme offering more details, and gave an address. So I wrote a letter and the papers started

coming. I told my husband and he said, 'Yes, why don't you go ahead and do it?' So I started in 1984.

My children were small then and I couldn't do a daytime course away from home. But the OU brochure said, you can do it on your own time, you can be your own boss. I had always wanted a bachelor's degree. I was good at studying, and I had worked very hard, so why didn't I have a degree?

You say you had worked very hard but didn't have a degree. Tell me about your prior education.

I was born in 1948 in a mountain village where everyone raised tea, 5,000 feet above sea level. I was an only child, although when I was 10 my parents adopted another daughter, who still lives in the village. Everybody has a plot of land and they look after their land, raise a bit of tea, coffee, cardamom, cinnamon, cloves. There was a very small village school where my grandparents went and my father went and I went. I began at age 4 and left at age 11 in 1959. At grade 5 they have a grammar school selection exam. I was 10 when I passed the 11-plus and got a scholarship to a grammar school, the Central College, a boarding-school. Both the village school and grammar school were mixed, boys and girls.

I was the only one in my class of twenty who passed. My mother pushed me to go to school as early as possible. My parents came from families that had many children and in my family I was the only one, so my parents were very obsessed that they should educate me.

The Central College was eight miles from my home. I was there from age 10 to 15, five years. I entered in 1959 and left in 1963. In grade 8, depending on your exam results, they stream you either for science, if you have good marks in sciences and maths, or you go in the commerce or the arts streams. I went into science and did O-levels in seven subjects. I was supposed to take eight subjects but I didn't take English because I didn't want to fail it. I took physics, chemistry, biology, mathematics, hygiene, Singhalese language and religion (Buddhism).

Now, if you wanted to do medicine A-levels, you had to have five O-level credits including English. So that was a bottleneck for me. I wanted to do medicine but I had studied everything in our mother tongue. Botany and zoology I learned very easily because I could go home on the weekend and find fresh specimens for everything we had in the lab in formalin. I was fascinated by the sciences and I wanted to be a doctor.

On my O-levels, I got 3 credits, one distinction, and 3 passes but I didn't have English. I didn't know what to do and my parents didn't have any idea either. If you don't pass your O-levels the first time, your scholarship stops. Another bottleneck. If you pass, then your scholarship is extended for two years for you to do A-levels. So I lost my scholarship. It was like the world had fallen in. I was worried, because studying at home and sitting for the whole exam again is very difficult, still I did it.

I repeated the exam in 1964 when I was 16 and got the 5 credits but still I didn't have English. I thought, I must learn English now. I stayed with a friend of my mother's in a different place and spent some time learning English with a tutor. I sat for my English and I just managed to get a pass.

Then in 1965 my parents took me to Colombo, our capital. They knew I wanted to be a doctor, so they spent a lot of money to send me to a good, private school. There most of the children spoke English so I heard English much of the time. I was there from 1965 to 1968 studying for four A-levels, physics, chemistry, botany and zoology. There was an English stream and a Singhalese stream in the school and I took my studies in Singhalese.

When you sat for the exam, first you did the theory paper and once you passed your theory, you were called for your practical. And when you have passed all four practicals, then if you wanted to do medicine, you had to do a special paper for organic chemistry and an organic practical in organic chemistry. You go all through this and then you are listed in terms of your qualifications. If the medical school has 150 seats, they take 150 and the rest are offered biological sciences. I was not selected for medicine. I repeated everything the next year and the following year, but I wasn't selected for medical school even though I'd passed my A-levels.

I didn't know what to do. Mind you, by the time I left Colombo in 1971, my English was pretty good. So I went to the village and they had a pupil teacher programme. You were a teacher for very low pay. I applied and I got my first appointment as a teacher. But when I saw the other two people who were selected, who had only done O-levels in the village and nothing after that, I was very disappointed, because now I had come down to that level. I was supposed to teach science and maths but, ironically, my English was so good I ended up as the English teacher!

In 1972 after I was married I lived in my parents' home and taught at the school. In 1973 and 1974 I went into teacher training at a specialist teachers' college and I specialized in sciences for secondary education. I did physics, chemistry, biology, educational psychology, methodology. So in 1974 after the exam I was qualified to teach a science curriculum.

What obstacles did you have to overcome in your OU studies?

I thought it would be child's play for me, so I started with the science foundation course. And it wasn't difficult except for the language because now I'm doing everything in English. They sent us a mini-lab and there were a lot of practicals to be done. I didn't have any problem with the practicals because in Sri Lanka I was in charge of the science laboratory. Therefore I knew all the apparatus, all the chemicals. Only the English language was a problem.

When I did my psychology course, my psychology lecturer always used to write in red ink something about my English. It kept reminding me that I was not up to standard. And it affected the grades that he gave me. So I talked to my tutor-counsellor and said, 'I don't want to go to this tutor anymore. I want my assignments to be graded by somebody else and I would like to have a different tutor.' She believed what I said and didn't question me. So I got a different person and I went to a different study group. My grades improved and the regrading was good.

When I came to England, things started going nice for me. Everyone was so kind. Even so, when I started my studies, I wanted to do courses that were familiar so that I didn't have to read a lot.

I never had a study partner or self-help group but the subjects I chose were so different that I never met the same people from year to year in my tutorials. Everyone was from all over London, we lived very far from each another. So we only met in the evening tutorials. I would have liked to have someone to study with, but I didn't.

What does the OU mean to you?

The OU gave me so much confidence. When you are in Sri Lanka, the English people who come to the country are only a certain set, and you think the English are really bright, brilliant in their jobs, and you always have high expectations of them. Then you come here and you meet all kinds of people and you no longer see them as brilliant, organized white people, whatever stereotypical image is in your mind of white people.

If I hadn't gone to the Open University, then my world would have been very small. At the Open University I met and studied with lots of students. You get feedback from all of them. And you make your world bigger and bigger. Otherwise your world is your immediate family and your work. And I am not a person who keeps quiet in a corner!

What impacts did the OU have on your career?

While I was taking S101 in 1984 I started volunteering where I now work. And half-way through, in July and August, I got sent to St Louis in the United States to learn about conflict resolution because I was one of the founding members of the project. There were 18 of us and I was the only Asian in the project at that time. I got back in September, but it went all right and I passed S101. So early on I learned I can work on the project *and* do the OU. More confidence.

I have been employed by the project since 1986. And while my OU degree had nothing to do with getting the job, I continued to develop confidence through the OU. I really discovered myself when I did two courses at the same time during my third pregnancy.

You work for the Newham Conflict and Change Project. How would you handle the Stratford School situation I've been reading about?

First I'd tell them, I have no vested interest in your problem. Then I'd explain the work we do and how people are given to positions, and how it is human nature not to want to lose, and to hold back. Then I would listen to both parties separately and then bring them together and ask them to work in little groups: brainstorm what your problems are and how to work them out, and then bring them all together and have them show each other what they have worked out. Then I'll get each person's opinion about what the other groups had worked out. Then I would ask him, 'What do you think about this? See what has been attained. You are saying this is wrong? Why do you think it is wrong? What are the other options?'

We have seen each others' problems, now is there a way you can resolve it without anyone losing? A solution has to come out of this, because otherwise there are consequences. If you don't resolve it, what are the consequences? What will happen to the children and the staff and the parents and the whole community? I believe we could handle Stratford. It is difficult when both groups are so polarized, but if they do not work it out, they will suffer the consequences.

My opinion is that religion should be taught at home. Schools should not have anything to do with religion. Or the students should learn about all religions without giving preference to one. If you can't do that, then take religion out of the curriculum. But I don't think it can happen here. One group says this is a Christian country, therefore we shouldn't have other religions taught in the schools. And other groups say, 'Why can't we have Christian and Muslim and Catholic schools?'

What is happening now is they want holidays for Id which is a Muslim festival and for Diwali, a Hindu festival, and the Sikh religion also has a birthday festival. So schools in different boroughs are open and closed on different dates for different holidays. Once you start, there is no end to it, that is what I am trying to say. So in this borough you get holidays for all these things. Then the children have to make up their holiday time at some other time.

And how do you resolve simple problems, like the noise complaints that happen all over London?

It's mainly the noise of children who live in flats, loud music, banging doors. Often we find that noise, the apparent problem, is not the underlying problem. Sometimes a complaint about noise is a cry for help, or the complainer just doesn't like that person, so he uses noise as the excuse. We don't take a problem at face value. We have trained mediators, we call them conciliators. If an Indian woman is in conflict with a white woman, we like to match the race of the volunteer conciliators with the clients. Or if one client is old and the other one is young, we match on that.

Lots of problems have gone on for years. And the people thought there wasn't anything they could do about it. What we normally do is get the people together and negotiate so that nobody wins or loses. Sometimes you get a very lonely woman or man who calls us to complain about noise. So you get a volunteer involved and the next time you phone them to ask how things are, they say, 'Since you visited it's okay'. And sometimes you haven't even visited yet!

What's the most important use you make of your OU degree?

Educating other people. There is this Western stereotype of Asian women that we are timid and do what we're told. So I like to mention some prominent women and disprove that myth about Asian women. For example, there was Indira Gandhi in India. And the first woman prime minister came from Sri Lanka much before Margaret Thatcher. Her name was Sirimavo Banderanaike. And if you think of Pakistan, there is Benazir Bhutto.

I also like to teach about our religions. Sri Lankans historically were very tolerant, although it is not like that there now. But as a Buddhist I was brought up to be very tolerant and treat other people as equals. Therefore this concept of equal opportunities, we grew up with it, we believed it as children. Every day when we went to school we recited these five precepts about not killing or hurting. Animals feel pain, therefore don't hurt them. In fact, Buddhists should not have a caste system because Buddhism was born out of Hinduism to fight the caste system. And because Hindus sacrifice animals to please their gods, Buddha said there is no god up there, it is all man-created. And Buddha said by birth nobody can be a high caste or a low caste and that you can only become a higher caste by your actions. These are some of the facts I like to teach others.

You have said you are Singhalese and your husband is Tamil.

While I was in Colombo I met my husband, who was in medical school. He was born in 1946. He always has looked more mature than myself and I always look younger than I am. He got his medical degree in 1970. He did help me in chemistry, he used to come home and teach me things. We were not lovers, I just knew him and liked him. Also he was a medical student, so I admired him. He's a Tamil, so I was forced to speak in English with him. But my people couldn't know about him.

In 1972 we got married. He's a Tamil and a Hindu. I'm a Singhalese and a Buddhist. So it was a controversial marriage. We got married in the registrar's office. In 1971, when I was 23 years old, my parents said if you are not studying, you have to get married. And they were looking for someone for me to marry, and proposals were coming home, so I had to tell them I had met this man. Of course, my mother started crying because of the difficulties she knew we'd have. Because in my village, Indian Tamils brought there by the British are the tea-pickers and people thought they were inferior.

In January 1975 I was given my first teaching appointment. Now when you go to teacher training you had to declare whether you are married or not, because your first appointment will be where your husband works. I was sent there but still we didn't live in the same house because he had not got an okay from his family. He lived with his mother. His father died when he was very young and he was very attached to his mother. He believed that his family might give their blessing and we might have a wedding. But it never happened. So in 1976 when his mother went back to Colombo, where he had a house, he told them that we were married and we moved into our own house in Jaffna in the north.

I'd like to ask how the OU was right for you?

Number one is flexibility because you can do it whenever you want. Number two, I like meeting different people. Each year is a totally unknown crowd. There was always a different group, different lecturers, at summer school a different lot, so all six years you meet different people. And I like to work in huge groups.

The OU was designed for me because of this flexibility. And also the organization. You know exactly when the summer school is. So you can plan it very well. You know when your tutorials are and when the assignments are due. You have a counsellor who is very understanding. But you need a lot of discipline. There were nights when I had to drag myself to the tutorials.

Describe how you fitted in your OU studies with your family life.

When the children went to school, I studied in the morning. That was the best time. About 12 o'clock I did my cooking. Then before the children came home, I studied some more. My family took me to summer schools, dropped me there, and came back to pick me up. I had a summer school for S101, M101, S202, and for chemistry and took them very seriously. In class I was very active, whereas in little groups when people talked about soap operas on the television, I was a very inactive participant. Summer schools were important because you didn't have to think about your family and you met people who were in the same boat and people from all different backgrounds.

What do women in general need to succeed at the OU?

Determination. You've got to believe in yourself: 'I can do it.' Women with low self-confidence shouldn't start with M101 or something like that. If you have doubts about your potential, the last thing you should do is start with a foundation course. Instead, you should do a short course that doesn't lead to a degree to get a feel for it.

How 'good' is your Open University degree?

I think it's much better than any other degree anywhere because you have to do everything yourself. If you are attending an ordinary university on a daily basis you have time to talk about things, meet other students, sort out your problems, and do your assignments in the library. It's not like that when you're all alone, and once a week you go to college. You have to be very, very disciplined. My science degree is very good because most of the practicals were very difficult. You have to set it up on your own and you have nobody to help you. And you have a deadline. At an ordinary university everything is there and lecturers are around to give you a hand. Even if it takes ten years to get an OU degree, I don't think that is bad.

What was most important in your life before the Open University and what is most important now after the OU?

My marriage and my children were most important and my priorities haven't changed. Before the OU it was very difficult for me to get a job without a British qualification. Everybody wanted to know if I had anything. Now with this degree in my hand, it gives me confidence. And through the OU I got a perspective on the education I had in the village school and I realized that I had a firm, basic education. My OU studies give me self-validation. I think it is much better than other degrees because it becomes a part of your life and if you can do it, you value yourself more at the end of it.

Tell me about your name.

My name, Janaki, was given me by my husband when we got married. It's our own tradition. Because I had another name, you see? But in Hindu mythology this name is the highest honour a woman can have. You know about the Rama and Sita stories? No? Well, there is this great epic drama in Hinduism where the two great characters are Rama and Sita. Another name for Sita is Janaki. Because her father is Jana, and Janaki means Jana's daughter. So this woman is famous for determination in almost anything and everything.

One of Janaki's determinations is that her children do not suffer any obstacles the education system here might throw in their way. Her eldest child, the first to go into the local comprehensive, was placed in 'lower ability' groups. Even though the family may have only enough money for one child to go to private school, it is being spent on this daughter. They hope they won't have to pay for private education for their secondborn, a son, and the baby girl, but if they need to, they will find the money somehow.

   Indira Gandhi. . . Sirimavo Banderanaike. . . Benazir Bhutto. . . Janaki Mahendran – all very determined women.

Chapter 25

Val Burke *From Housewife to Computer Product Specialist*

From his occupational guidance job, my husband got to recognize what people might be good at, and he said I'd make a wonderful computer programmer. And while I was doing the science founda- tion course the OU started these computing courses and he said, 'I'll buy you a home computer if you want to do this'. So I applied and I got quite addicted. And I am quite certain that my OU studies were the key to my getting this job. First, having done well gave me greater confidence in my abilities; second, the fact that I was studying with the OU helped me show initiative to the people interviewing; and third, the computing courses gave me useful background knowledge.

Val said on the phone that she was five feet five inches tall and would be wearing glasses. Not much to go on. But I instantly recognized her in the Sheffield BR foyer, as she did me – five feet seven inches and also wearing glasses. We shook hands and headed for the carpark.

It was Saturday, but Val was dressed for work. Long, dark-blue skirt and top, high heels, a casual, modish beige jacket as protection from the bitter February wind. A quick drive to her semi-detached house in a part of town known as Totley. There I met her husband, Tom, who made the two of us tea and then disappeared to do the weekly shopping.

She settled across from me at a table in their front room, shoulder-length auburn hair patted back into place, cheeks bright from the wind, red lips sipping from a mug. Val speaks in short, clipped sentences. She gives the impression of a no-nonsense, serious professional, not a hint of housewife about her. In fact, she hates housework.

Val was born in Leeds in 1955. She has two brothers, both engineers, and a sister. Val's father is a retired mechanical engineer who worked for Lucas Aerospace. Her mother was also a mature student who qualified as a teacher when Val was in her teens. This is what Val wrote to me in February 1991:

I am married, with two children, girls aged 13 and 15 years, and I shall be 36 years old next month. I did not work at all while my children were growing up, and my initial reason for studying with the OU was to have something interesting to do during the day when my husband and the children were out all day at school or work. However, during my fifth year of study I began to feel that my degree, when I completed it, would be useful in helping me start a career so I started feeling quite excited about future prospects.

I started studying the Maths foundation course in 1985, then followed this up with a Pure Maths course followed by the Science foundation course. The course that made the big difference to my life was Fundamentals of Computing, which I studied in 1988, the year it was introduced. This course is an introduction to computing and computers, and involves using a PC at home to do some programming and also to perform various practical activities to follow up the ideas introduced in the course. I enjoyed this course so much that I followed it up in 1989 with two half-credit courses, both of which were about computing. During the summer of that year I noticed that the Regional Health Authority were looking for trainee computer programmers to work in their computer department, so, encouraged by my husband, I applied for the job. Imagine my surprise and pleasure when I was offered my first-ever job!

What were your reasons for pursuing an OU degree?

I was just sitting at home, getting very bored, nothing to do, no real prospect of doing any more than carrying on, sitting at home. I suppose my mother's example might have helped, because she left school at 16, went to work for a few years, got married, had kids and was at home for quite a few years before she left for teacher training college. She was bored with her life as well. She went full-time for two years to get her certificate, and she says she was quite often up late at night writing essays. I was 16, 17 at the time but I can't remember much of her studying at all.

I don't know if lazy is the right word, but I thought, if I did the OU degree, I could do it at home so I wouldn't have to stir myself to go out. Even though I felt myself stuck in all the time. I thought it would put my brain in action but I could still be here when the children came home from school. If they were sick, no problems, I was here. It was a gentle introduction to whatever I wanted a gentle introduction to.

We moved to Sheffield eight years ago, in 1984, to this house, and a lady over the road, she was doing a university degree in environmental science, having started with the OU. She told me how much she enjoyed herself and I started thinking, there *is* more to life than this. So I sent off for all the stuff and applied and got accepted. But I didn't think, Oh, if I do this, I'll get a job when I've finished it.

What obstacles did you have to succeeding at the OU?

I wasn't aware of any to start with, because Tom has always been very supportive. And the girls very quickly got the idea that when I was studying, they had got to keep quiet, and turn the radio off. Once I started work, it got harder. If it was a nice sunny Sunday, I couldn't go out and sit in the garden. I'd got to come in here and get the books out. It was a struggle, but I never had the difficulties some people did. Some women's husbands didn't want them to do it. Or they don't have the money to do it.

For one of the courses the tutorial was in Leeds, this was before we bought the car, so I didn't go to any of those. Depending on how many people are doing a course, they have tutorials in most of the big towns in a region, or just one tutorial in one town in each region. So if there are not many people doing a particular course in the Yorkshire region, the tutorial will be in Leeds. Leeds is about 30 miles away. So that was an obstacle. It was my first computing course and I had to manage without going.

Obviously the subject of maths was not an obstacle for you as it is for many women, starting in secondary school.

After the 11-plus, most of us in Wolverhampton where I grew up went on to the same mixed comprehensive which took all abilities. But once you got there you were streamed according to ability based on the 11-plus results. I was in the top stream, all the way through.

I've always liked maths and numbers and I've never liked writing essays. The way they organized the choices, you had to do certain subjects. Then you could pick one or two others. Then depending on what you picked, that restricted you on your last two subjects. O-levels I did in maths, physics, English literature, English language, history, biology, French, chemistry. I did A-levels in maths, physics and economics.

Many women get put off maths in school. If you're at school and you get the feeling that you can't do maths, you end up being frightened of it and don't want to do it. Everybody had to do O-level maths so there was a better proportion of girls there, but in every A-level maths class at school, there were more boys than girls. Today my daughter finds it very confusing doing maths. When you see her exam results, she's doing fine, but she feels as though she is struggling with it. A lot depends on the teacher. She's taking GCSE this year and everybody has to do maths. They did some mock exams and her teacher hadn't got them as far as he should have done. There were questions she should have been able to answer that she couldn't because they'd not yet done the work. So now she feels maths is not for her.

What does the Open University mean to you?

It's a chance to get out and do something to help yourself. If I had never started on that degree, I probably wouldn't be working now. Well, perhaps I would be working, but I wouldn't have such an interesting job with such good prospects. If I'd not done this degree, I'd just have the A-levels I had when I was 18.

It changes you, doing it. It wakes you up. I was at home, not doing much, not exercising my brain, and then I started having confidence in myself. You find you can do it, and you say, What can I do next? So I wrote off to apply for this job. I was doing the OU so I had got something to offer. I was interviewed by two people who worked here in computing and one person from personnel and they asked me questions about what I'd been studying. I had to explain the OU to them. People have a great deal of difficulty grasping that you can do different subjects, sometimes unrelated subjects, and still get a degree. Then they asked me what did I think working as a team meant, and would I like working with other people. All I could say was, 'I'm really terrified! This is the only job interview I've ever had.'

Can you give me some other examples of your greater confidence?

It got started at summer school. Some students used to stay in their rooms in the evenings studying. I didn't. I'm not all that sociable when I'm at home, but being away in strange surroundings, you've got to make the effort and you do. To stay in your room when you knew there were things going on elsewhere, and not see anybody, is not what summer school is for. It's to meet other people and see how they are getting along in the course. So

I got a bit more self-confidence out of that, that I could go out, walk into a room full of strangers, and talk.

And like I said, when I saw this job advertised with Trent Regional Health Authority, they wanted trainee computer programmers if you'd got to the degree level. But I thought, if you don't write off and ask for things, you'll never get them, so I said I wasn't finished with my OU degree yet but I'd like to apply anyway. First of all, they sent me for the aptitude test. Quite a lot of people did the aptitude tests and they got the results of those and whittled the numbers down. And then interviewed some people. I wasn't their first choice but they took on five people altogether. So I started October 1989. We have been privatized so we are part of AT&T ISTEL now.

I suppose the most recent example of my self-confidence is I've started going to the gym three times a week. If you weren't visiting, I'd be at the gym right now. The instructors work out exercise programmes for everybody, lifting weights, cycling, stair-walker, aerobics. I started doing this eight months ago because I could feel flabby, unhealthy unfitness creeping over me from sitting at a desk all day. I've never done anything like this before. And I am more fit. We've been decorating Sarah's bedroom and we've got this plastic, mix-it-yourself stuff for the walls and Tom was trying to mix it and getting nowhere, so I just took the stick and stirred it round, and he tried it again, and he couldn't move it. So I am stronger than I used to be.

Tell me about your career.

People at work at first didn't realize how much time and commitment it takes to do an OU degree. They've all got degrees in computing or accountancy. It's come up because I've had to explain each year that I needed to go to an exam. So I made sure they knew I was doing it. And they've asked me how my exams have gone, each time I've done that.

I haven't had the experience and haven't done as much as the others on my team, but ability-wise, I'm as good as them. At some things I might be better, for example, sometimes I see what a program's doing better and faster than the men. The OU computing and programming courses gave me more practice at that way of thinking.

For the science foundation course you had to do essays. And for one of the computing courses which has more to do with theory, you had to write long answers to questions. From writing those essays and questions, I learned what needs to go into reports and how to be concise. I have done one short report so far, about training people in Chesterfield in the pre-school module.

After my training I worked at writing new programs for the Trent Regional Health Authority breast-screening system. I wasn't a trainee any more and my wages increased. There were three of us on that and there wasn't quite enough work for three, so I am now on a team supporting a child health system.

Within the breast-screening system, women over 50 would be registered and sent an appointment for an initial visit. Then they'd go along for an initial check-up at various hospitals and clinics around the region, have their examination and mammography, and if there's anything suspicious that needs further investigation, they will be sent another appointment for assessment, and if there's nothing wrong, they'll be told they're okay.

So the computer program was to get the women registered, make the appointments, record the results, and record whether or not they need to be sent for again, and produce the letters and postcards and other documents.

The child health system where I'm working now has a lot more to it, starting with registering the children on the system at birth: name and address, GP, health visitor. They record the mother onto the system, mother's antenatal details, child's measurements at birth, birth weight, any physical problems with the baby, any complications, any drugs given to the mother. Some sites record the parents' occupations, some don't; some record the ethnic origin, some don't.

I do a lot of heavy thinking during the day. I usually go to work at 8.20, get to work about twenty to nine, take 35 minutes for lunch and leave about 5. Everybody in our house gets their own breakfast, Sarah and Judy get their own tea – toasted cheese sandwiches or frozen pizzas – they get their lunch at school, and I do dinner for Tom and me when I get home, but it's usually convenience food out of the freezer. Tom washes up, somebody feeds the washing machine, Tom does my ironing for me, the girls do their own ironing. I don't do housework at all until it's got to the state where I can't relax. So then I do the whole house and forget it for a week or two.

What is the most important use you make of your OU degree?

I use it most when I do training courses. This year I'll probably get Customer Care. They're teaching me how to train customers, that is, medical administrators, to use the system. At the moment there are these various different modules to this child health system. And not every site has got every module. So every now and then one of our sites takes on a new module, and we have to go and show them how it works.

The computer department is now privatized and with private companies somebody's got to go out and actively sell the products. We haven't got a captive audience. There are other companies selling similar products so we've got to do a good job of persuading people ours is a lovely product. The people in charge at a customer site are educated to degree level. They are managers and have quite a bit of responsibility. But the actual people who get everyday hands-on experience vary from clerks on up. So we train everybody from the clerk to the degreed manager. Last year I trained in Chesterfield, where they will start using the pre-school module. It was two days, one day in October, one in November. I was terrified, nervous for days before. I didn't feel very confident, but they understood what I told them and everything went all right.

I work with three men and we're part of a bigger team, and what happens is, the customer has a problem, so they ring up the service desk and say, 'We've got a problem with this.' So the service desk brings it up to the office and the person who is not doing anything at the time looks at it. He might get on with it and fix it, or we work as a team if we've picked up a call that we can't sort out.

I also used my OU studies to write a completely fresh program for the child health. Programming involves getting the customer to pay for it. And they haven't always got the spare money. I created a small program for one of the sites that wanted to keep the ethnic origin of the children and the birth weight, so they just wanted a little program that would enable them to go through everybody and pick up these two bits of information for the children's records and correct it.

What I'm doing now as a product specialist is supporting. Users ring up and say we've got a problem with this, that and the other, and we go away and play around with the program and find out the cause of the problem. *That is nice*, chasing up a problem, and getting a program to do what it's supposed to.

My Graphs, Networks and Design course will be useful if I ever reach the stage of planning a project. Project planning would be developing and creating new programs.

How have you balanced your OU studies with your other responsibilities?

The first five years I was at home all day. The kids were at school. So between 9 o'clock and half past 3, if I felt like studying, I did. But if I hadn't studied in the day, I'd sit round in the evening studying, and everybody knew that Mummy's studying, we'd better keep quiet. I had the occasional week where I didn't feel like doing anything and if there was an assignment, on Sunday I'd have to sit down and do it. But most of the studying was done during the week when everybody was out of the house.

I got the results of my last OU course just before Christmas and I managed to pass it, Graphs, Networks and Design. The work I'm doing now is so demanding I was always tired when I got home in the evening, too tired to really get into it, so I was struggling a bit. But April the fourth I'll get my degree.

What do you think is the most important ingredient in women-in-general's success at the OU?

In spite of the struggle you can't give up. Once you get some confidence and a goal, you've got to finish. When I was 18 I didn't know what I wanted to do. We used to have chats with careers officers and they would always suggest, 'Oh, you could do this or you could do that.' But I'd think, I can't do that, I can't do the other. And the teachers all said, 'You could go to university, why don't you?' So I did because I couldn't think of anything better to do. I went to Leeds and studied Economics but I kept failing all my exams. I was drifting. And at that age I never felt I'd *got* to do something.

It also helps to have a supportive husband. I remember an Asian lady about 21, doing the maths foundation course summer school. She'd got a small baby. We got on quite well that week and she was surprised that I talked to her. She seemed to believe that because she wasn't white, people wouldn't talk to her. And the second year when I went to Reading, she was at that summer school as well. What's more, she was doing two courses that year. And coping with a family and a husband who thought she ought to stay at home. When she was home she had to wear traditional-type Indian clothes because he was very traditional, but at summer school she wore Western clothes and used to come drinking with us in the evenings.

What was the hardest part of your OU studies and the easiest part?

I think one of the best parts were the summer schools. I only did three because not every course had a summer school. The first was the maths foundation course in Reading. I'd been very nervous about going away and meeting lots of strange people. It hadn't sunk in that everybody was going to be in the same situation and not know anybody. So I finally relaxed and met other people and some of the time we worked in small groups of a dozen or so, and you got to know everybody in the group and found people to go round with. Evenings I'd go sit and chat in the bar.

The units themselves made it easy, they were excellent. There was everything in them that you needed to know. They take you so gradually into things. You start off doing something easy and after a bit you realize it's got quite complicated, but I found I was still with it. They recommended to people doing the maths foundation course that they first go through a couple of textbooks as a sort of basic refresher, not much beyond O-level standard. Statistics, algebra, geometry, a little introduction to calculus. You didn't have to do it, but because I had such a long wait between applying, getting a place and starting, I did it and I'd recommend it.

What quality, in addition to aptitude for maths, made you succeed at the OU?

I don't like giving up. There are times when you're too tired to do an assignment when it's due. So you say, 'Right, it's due, so I'll just sit down and get on with it.' I just forced myself.

Also, I wanted to do a good job. I've never liked doing a slapdash job, just dash off an assignment, particularly with the maths, because I enjoyed it, so I always tried to get the right answer out. I might spend several hours or even days over it. Just to do a good job and not give up on it.

You do have to be able to work on your own. Funnily enough now something I do miss from going to work is peace and quiet. There's never a chance to sit down, and know that for two or three hours you can just curl up with a book and not be disturbed. You don't appreciate peace and quiet until you've lost it. I try to take my leave so that I can have a week or two at a time, so I can read to my heart's content.

The Burkes enjoy living in tiny Totley with its grey stone farm buildings and old schoolhouse. A multi-storey hall of residence for Sheffield Polytechnic tries to dominate the scene, but the eye moves to far-away grey-green hills and dark hedgerows, mossy stone walls, distant square church towers. I asked about retirement. They would like to move 15 miles away to an even smaller village and better vistas.

The inside of Val's house was in the state of a major overhaul. The outside of the house had already been refurbished, new stucco, new roof, new gutters, new doors and windows. The interior walls had been replastered and were waiting for wallpaper and paint. Her new kitchen windows look out on a long, weed-choked garden with lots of debris that will need to be carried away. Now that the OU is but a memory, Val can turn to gardening when she isn't curled up with a good book, having a bit of peace and quiet. As she says:

> 'It's nice not to have to ask Tom for money whenever I need anything. I just go out and spend the money. We are doing the house up, which we couldn't do before I started work. We have done the outside and now we're doing the inside. The roof needed work, the windows were going, the gutters were full of holes. When you're at home all the time, it gets you down when you see all this stuff that needs doing and you haven't got the money. So it's great to be able to say now, Right, let's start on this room next.'

Chapter 26

The OU: Undoing Educational Obstacles

The OU is the university that comes to you. Whether you live in a big city, a small market town, a country village, on a remote farm or even an oil rig, the courses you take will have the same high-quality content and will be taught to the same high standards. (*Guide to the BA Degree Programme*, 1993)

In a nutshell, what is the OU?

The Open University was established by Royal Charter in 1969 and is now Britain's largest single teaching institution. Two names stand out in its history, Harold Wilson and Jennie Lee. When Wilson became Prime Minister in 1964 he asked Jennie Lee, his Minister for the Arts, to oversee the 'University of the Air' project. It was she who eventually won over Wilson's Cabinet and made the OU a reality. In 1971 the first 24,000 undergraduates were admitted.

Today the OU serves 125,000 registered students and an equal number who buy self-contained study packs for one of the OU's courses. Thus, at any point in time, over 200,000 men and women are OU students. By 1992 the OU had awarded 115,000 bachelor's degrees.

The OU has a worldwide reputation for the quality of its courses and the effectiveness of its distance-teaching methods. Every course is designed for students learning on their own and uses specially produced textbooks organized into units. These units are linked to other distance materials: radio and television programmes, audio and video tapes, home experiment kits, computer software and local tuition and counselling. Courses have a three-hour final exam, and external assessors ensure that OU standards are the same as at other British universities.

The OU has 13 regional centres which oversee 5,700 tutors and counsellors in the UK and Europe. The centres organize tutorials, day schools, summer schools and exams. Every undergraduate attends at least one summer school, which lasts a week. These are held on university campuses around the UK in the vacation months. Students also have a local tutor and counsellor, whom they see regularly at group tutorial meetings at one of the 250 study centres throughout the UK.

The OU is open to anybody. There are no entry qualifications required, no tests to take, no grades to have been earned, no barriers of any kind. Admission is on a first-come first-served basis. Limits of staff and resources govern how many students can be admitted and then accepted on each course, so there are quotas and waiting lists. In spite of the open entry policy, 80 per cent of finally registered undergraduates successfully complete their first-year exams, and more than 55 per cent of them graduate four, five, six or more years later.

To gain a BA, OU students must complete six credits. Each course lasts nine months (February to October) and typically it takes six years to get a BA. Everyone starts with a foundation course. Then students can do another foundation course, or choose from 130 other courses at second, third and fourth level. In November 1992 the University Senate created a BSc degree and honours degrees based on six rather than eight credits.

Students put together the kind of BA that best suits their interests and needs. Some people concentrate on one narrow area, some people take wild smatterings of many different courses. After the foundation course, students can take breaks of a year or more and resume their studies when they want to.

The OU is an inexpensive form of higher education, for both the government and individual student. For the government, OU costs per undergraduate degree are 40 per cent less than at conventional universities. For the student, the cost per course in 1993, including a summer school, was only £407.

What do we know about OU students?

1. Almost half are women, the highest proportion of women students of any UK university.
2. The majority are in their late twenties, thirties or forties. The youngest are in their late teens, the oldest in their nineties.
3. Three out of four students are in paid employment throughout their studies.
4. One in five students starting undergraduate study has the minimum two A-levels needed for other universities; nearly half have no A-levels at all.
5. Half had fathers in blue-collar occupations (compared to one in five at conventional universities).

While more than half of the women you got to know in this book came from working-class backgrounds, at the time they did the OU they were all living in comfortable circumstances. In fact, mature students tend to be middle-class rather than working-class.

The largest age group entering the OU in 1990–91 was 30 to 39 years old (38%); 34% were 29 and younger, and 28% were 40 and over (Woodley, 1992). In our group of fourteen, four started the OU in their twenties, six in their thirties and four in their forties. Likewise, compared to women starting the OU in 1990–91, of whom approximately 40% were not in paid work, five of the fourteen (36%) were not in paid work when they did the OU. The group was less well qualified than recent OU undergraduates, of whom 50 per cent lacked the requisite two A-levels for conventional universities (Woodley, 1992). Only three of the fourteen women (Val, Janaki and Viv) had gained two A-levels.

What is the women's main advice for returners?

There are many lessons in this book for returners, whether they are 18 or 80, but the following advice bears repeating.

1.   **Get ready before starting the OU.** Teresa got ready by taking a preparatory course through the National Extension College and reading books on organizing one's time. Val got ready by reviewing her textbooks for A-levels in mathematics. And Dale, still in her cautious phase, did five GCE O-levels in English literature, English language, sociology, mathematics and psychology at Wakefield College of Arts and Technology.

It may be a blessing in disguise if you don't get into the OU immediately and must wait a year. That year should be packed with preparation, guaranteeing that you will have a fabulous foundation course experience because you will have established your private study space and practised using it on a regular basis.

2.   **Take courses for their intrinsic interest and the challenge.** OU women students, more than OU men, are motivated to try the unknown, the totally different. If science is missing from your life, follow Teresa and Frances and begin with the science foundation course. If you feel disadvantaged in mathematics, like Pauline and Ellen, take maths. If the world of painting, music and architecture begs to be illuminated, start with the arts foundation course, as Helen did.

But if improving your job performance is paramount, perhaps it would be enhanced by psychology and sociology, as our nurses, Editha and Gertrude, found out. Enter new territory when it suits.

3.   **Speak up in tutorials and don't be afraid to ask questions.** Shirleen Stibbe carried this lesson into her workplace where as an actuary-in-training, she delighted in constantly asking for clarification. And as an OU tutor, she expects her students to phone at any hour. Pauline agrees; you shouldn't be scared about phoning your tutor. Tutors will tell you if they can't talk at the moment and tell you when they can.

There are 6,000 of them out there and their job is to answer your questions. A good thing to remember is that tutors are also mature students, always learning more about their area of expertise, and about teaching, examining, problem-solving, small group dynamics and, last but not least, about you as a unique learner. They aren't afraid to ask questions. Neither should you be.

Edith also overcame her fears about asking questions, even though that first year she felt her group was operating at such a low level that it wasn't appropriate for them to ask their tutor *everything*. But it was appropriate to ask one another. Which brings us to Lesson Number 4.

4.   **Always find a study partner and participate in study groups.** Pauline couldn't believe her luck in the maths foundation course when she found that a very nice woman called Tania lived just around the corner. They did everything on that course together and took another mathematics course as well before going their separate ways. But Pauline learned to always look around her technological classes for another woman to team up with.

Editha says her groups were formed on the basis of proximity and met in one anothers' homes. Frances says her partners had to be phone partners because rural students live so far apart, but it worked anyway. Janaki regretted that her classes were filled with people from all over London so that she never had the support of a small study group.

But everyone recognized that study partners and support groups generally facilitate learning. Small groups are one more way to succeed at the OU and well worth your organizing.

5.   Go to summer school. Some of the women you've met deliberately chose courses that did not involve a summer school; others chose courses *because* they had summer schools. I think you should choose your courses because they are what you want to take. But if two possibilities are equally appealing and one has a summer school, take that one. Why?

Summer school is an essential part of the OU. Summer school can be so powerful, so awesome, so intense a learning experience, that students have a hard time describing it. All Viv knew was that this was what she should have done when she was 18 – live on campus and find out who she really was.

6.   Accept that you don't have to do everything. Pauline and Tania took one look at the maths foundation summer school and said, 'We'll go nuts if we try to do all they're asking of us. So let's pick and choose and then relax and have a good time.' It worked.

Kushalta found that she could skip entire TMAs and not fail. She didn't like doing this, but when a crisis strikes, there are ways not to drop out and get through a course. Val discovered she could miss all the tutorials and still succeed, while Janaki found she could be out of the country for two months and pass her exam. And Ellen found she didn't have to do any recommended reading and could get by. She now believes it was a mistake, and vows she'll never do it again, but you can get through your course without doing all the extras.

Accepting that you don't have to do everything connected with a course is, ironically, part of gaining control over your learning.

7.   Don't miss any opportunity. Isn't this antithetical to Lesson Number 6? Not really. See all the opportunities around you and then decide when you'll seize them.

In the matter of careers, for example, Frances never missed a chance to consult with an OU counsellor. Misha, on the other hand, noticed that career counselling was available, but put it off until she spotted a regular university advisory office and walked in. Pauline delayed until she had her degree and could put her BA on her CV before getting career guidance.

But all three received support and encouragement. All three got headed in the right direction. And all three now trust professional career counsellors and would use them in the future.

As Ellen said, working 9 to 5 'isn't it. There are loads of things that can crop up that you can do. And you don't ever want to say, No.'

8.   Link up your OU degree with your future career as soon as possible. You may begin your OU degree with the same tentativeness, fears and lack of career goals as these

OU women did. But the sooner you begin to ask how your OU studies do relate, and can relate, to your career, the better.

For what you want to do, is a pass degree or an honours degree advisable? For the job of management consultant, Misha found out almost too late. For the training you need, should you apply for other programmes before or after your OU degree? For the job of dentist, Ellen found out just in time. For the job of cytogeneticist, should you take chemistry or physics or some other science? Teresa says it didn't matter, just as long as she had an honours science degree. Cytogeneticists get trained on the job.

And never forget Val, our computer specialist, who began her first-ever job *before* she finished her OU degree. The two dovetailed together perfectly. There was no reason to delay until she was finished with the OU.

9.   Don't give up when you get discouraged – everyone gets discouraged. The hardest part, they all said, was being tired and overwhelmed by an assignment and having to sit yourself down anyway, and do it. Who can forget Editha's husband reading to her as she stood at the ironing board? Who can forget Misha's temptation to give up and not send in all her assignments? Remember Shirleen's husband saying, 'You felt the same way last year at this time. Go on, you can do it.' Remember that summer school is a built-in cure for mid-course blues. You go fed up and prepared to pack it in, and come home ready to take your final exam.

Or when you get discouraged, find this book and read your favourite story over again.

10.   Remember: we're all disabled and we're all especially abled. All OU students have obstacles to overcome. Some are more obvious than others, such as being in a wheelchair or having a guide-dog. But having a resistant spouse, or enormous child responsibilities, or a death in the family – or *not* having enough money, or a car to drive to tutorials, or a supportive boss, are disabling as well.

Rather than dwell on your obstacles, think of yourself as your greatest resource. And recall what the women said is the most important characteristic for succeeding at the OU: Determination to finish what you start. Discipline. Perseverance. Sheer terrier-like persistence.

And the address is: Admissions Office, The Open University, Milton Keynes MK7 6AA.

References

Baird, Janet (1992) Brutal facts of prowess. *Guardian Education*, 20 October, p.4.

Baird, Janet (1993) Over-age outcasts. *Guardian Education*, 26 January, p.5.

Berridge, Kate (1992) From smart young gel to power-pupil. *Independent on Sunday*, 6 September, p.18.

Blackstone, Tessa (1992) The full cost of part-time maturity. *Guardian*, 11 February, p.21.

Bolton, Eric (1992) Visions of chaos. *Times Educational Supplement*, 31 July, p.10.

Brown, Phillip (1989) Schooling for inequality? Ordinary kids in school and the labour market. In Ben Cosin, Mike Flude and Margaret Hales (eds), *School, Work and Equality*. London: Hodder & Stoughton.

Buckley, Kevin (1992) The iron curtain that has divided Dartford. *Guardian Education*, 8 December, p.7.

Burgess, Averil (1990) Co-education – the disadvantages for schoolgirls. *Gender and Education*, 2, pp. 91–5.

Buxton, Alexandra (1993) How a friendship ended. *Guardian Education*, 2 February, pp. 4–5.

Chubb, John and Moe, Terry (1992) How to get the best from Britain's schools. *Sunday Times Magazine*, 9 February, p.18.

Cole, Martina (1993) My essays were a write-off; today I'm a writer. *Independent*, 7 January, p.15.

Cornbleet, Annie and Libovitch, Sue (1983) Anti-sexist initiatives in a mixed comprehensive school: A case study. In Ann-Marie Wolpe and James Donald (eds), *Is There Anyone Here from Education?* London: Pluto Press.

Corrigan, Paul (1992) The politics of Access courses in the 1990s. *Journal of Access Studies*, 7, pp.19–32.

Coward, Rosalind (1993) Bringing them up to be bigots. *The Observer Review*, 18 July, p.45.

Davies, Joan (1991) Agenda. *Guardian*, 10 September, p.21.

Davies, Kath, Dickey, Julienne and Stratford, Teresa (eds) (1987) *Out of Focus: Writing on Women and the Media*. London: The Women's Press.

Deem, Rosemary and Finch, Janet (1986) Claiming our space: Women in a 'Socialist Alternative' post-18 education. In Janet Finch and Michael Rustin (eds), *A Degree of Choice: Education after Eighteen*. Harmondsworth: Penguin.

Department for Education (1992) *The Preparation of Girls for Adult and Working Life*. London: HMI.

Department of Education and Science (1991) *Education Statistics for the United Kingdom, 1990 Edition*. London: HMSO.

Edwards, Rosalind (1990) Access and assets: the experience of mature mother-students in higher education. *Journal of Access Studies*, 5, pp.188–202.

Evans, Mary (1991) *A Good School: Life at a Girls' Grammar School in the 1950s*. London: The Women's Press.

Fitzgerald, Penelope (1978) *The Bookshop*. London: Flamingo.

French, Jane (1990) *The Education of Girls: A Handbook for Parents*. London: Cassell.

Garner, Anne (1990) Stepping out: a mature student's view of higher education. *Journal of Access Studies*, 5, pp.218–20.

Giles, Judy (1990) Second chance, second self? *Gender and Education*, 2, pp.357–61.

Girls widen school lead over boys and catch up at colleges. *Guardian*, 23 January 1992, p.5.

Hanna, Lynn (1992) Workers elect a fair deal. *Guardian*, 21 January, p.16.

Heron, Liz (ed.) (1985), *Truth, Dare or Promise: Girls Growing up in the Fifties*. London: Virago.

Holdsworth, Angela (1988) *Out of the Dolls's House*. London: BBC Books.

Hughes, Mary and Kennedy, Mary (eds) (1985) *New Futures: Changing Women's Education*. London: Routledge & Kegan Paul.

Hymas, Charles and Nelson, Francesca (1992) Life at the bottom. *The Sunday Times*, 22 November, p.13.

Ingham, Mary (1981) *Now We Are Thirty: Women of the Breakthrough Generation*. London: Eyre Methuen.

Jack, Marion (1987) SOLE – The Strathclyde Open Learning Experiment. In Mary Thorpe and David Grugeon (eds), *Open Learning for Adults*. Harlow: Longman.

Kelly, Jean (1991) A study of gender differential linguistic interaction in the adult classroom. *Gender and Education*, 3, pp.137–43.

Lonsdale, Sarah (1993) Why can't an Oxbridge woman be more like a man? *Observer*, 1 August, p.57.

Lowe, Catharine (1992) Science subject to sexual politics. *The Sunday Observer Magazine*, 2 February, p.13.

Lowman, Roger (1992) Left behind in the crush. *Times Educational Supplement Review*, 27 November, p.6.

McGiffen, Steve (1993) Playing in Europe – at home and away. *Guardian Education*, 2 March, p.7.

MacIntosh, Margaret (1990) Second-time pupils: The return of women to school. In Judith Fewell and Fiona Paterson (eds), *Girls in Their Prime: Scottish Education Revisited*. Edinburgh: Scottish Academic Press.

McLaren, Arlene T. (1985) *Ambitions and Realizations: Women in Adult Education*. London: Peter Owen.

Mahony, Pat (1992) Which way forward? Equality and schools in 1991. *Women's Studies International Forum*, 15, pp.293–302.

Meikle, James (1992) Praise bias for boys in school. *Guardian*, 10 February, p.5.

Millard, Jeremy (1985) Local tutor–student contact in the Open University. *Teaching at a Distance*, 26, pp.11–22.

Myers, Kate (1992) Keeping the customers satisfied. *Times Educational Supplement Review*, 27 November, p.5.

Nicholson, Joyce (1980) *What Society Does to Girls*. London: Virago.

Perry, Baroness (1992) Prospects poor for women. *Guardian Education*, 17 November, p.4.

Pratt, John (1985) The attitudes of teachers. In Judith Whyte, Rosemary Deem, Lesley Kant and Maureen Cruickshank (eds), *Girl-Friendly Schooling*. London: Methuen.

Purvis, June (1991) *A History of Women's Education in England*. Milton Keynes: Open University Press.

Sex equality. *Guardian*, 18 November 1992, p.11.

Spear, Margaret Goddard (1985) Teachers' attitudes towards girls and technology. In Judith Whyte, Rosemary Deem, Lesley Kant and Maureen Cruickshank (eds), *Girl-Friendly Schooling*. London: Methuen.

Spender, Dale (1984) Sexism in teacher education. In Sandra Acker and David Piper (eds), *Is Higher Education Fair to Women?* Guildford: SRHE, NFER/Nelson.

Sperling, Liz (1989) *Barriers to Women Participating in Higher Education*, Departmental Paper No. 23, Department of Politics and Contemporary History, University of Salford.

Sperling, Liz (1991) Can the barriers be breached? Mature women's access to higher education. *Gender and Education*, 3, pp. 199–215.

Strickland, Sarah (1992) Profit and loss of opting for selection. *Independent on Sunday*, 9 February, p.11.

Suleiman, Leila and Suleiman, Susan (1985) Mixed blood – that explains a lot of things. In Gaby Weiner (ed.), *Just a Bunch of Girls: Feminist Approaches to Schooling*. Milton Keynes: Open University Press.

Sweetman, Jim (1992) Second among equals. *Guardian Bulletin*, 25 February, p.19.

Thane, Philip (1992) Chained to a father's pursestrings. *Times Educational Supplement Review*, 25 September, p.6.

Thomas, Kim (1990) *Gender and Subject in Higher Education*. Buckingham: Open University Press.

Thomas, Susan (1992) My best teacher: Tessa Sanderson talks to Susan Thomas. *Times Educational Supplement Review*, 27 November, p.2.

Thompson, Jane L. (1983a) *Learning Liberation: Women's Responses to Men's Education*. London: Croom Helm.

Thompson, Jane (1983b) Women and Adult Education. In Malcolm Tight (ed), *Education for Adults, II: Educational Opportunities for Adults*. London: Croom Helm.

Universities' Statistical Record (1991) *University Statistics 1989–90: Students and Staff*, Cheltenham: USR.

Walshe, John (1992) No profit for girls in mixed company. *Times Educational Supplement*, 23 October, p.17.

Ward, David (1992) The red rose graduates. *Guardian Education*, 15 December, pp.2–3.

Weil, S.W. (1986) Non-traditional learners within traditional higher education institutions: discovery and disappointment. *Studies in Higher Education*, 11, pp.219–35.

Wheeler-Bennett, Joan (1977) *Women at the Top*. London: Peter Owen.

White, Lesley (1992) Interview with Margaret Beckett. *Sunday Times*, 19 January, Section 2, p.3.

Wickham, Ann (1986) *Women and Training*. Milton Keynes: Open University Press.

Women's Monitoring Network (1987) Sugar and spice – how the media stereotype children. In Kath Davies, Julienne Dickey and Teresa Stratford (eds), *Out of Focus: Writings on Women and the Media*. London: The Women's Press.

Woodley, Alan (1992) *The Ethnic Origin of Open University Students and Staff*, Student Research Centre Report No. 63. Milton Keynes: Open University.

Young, Susan (1992) Choice widens class divide. *Times Educational Supplement*, 2 October, p.8.

Selected Resources

Judith Bell, Sheila Hamilton and Gordon Roderick (1986) *Mature Students: Entry to Higher Education*. London: Longman. How to go about choosing subjects, chances of being accepted, how to apply for places and prepare for admission, finding the money. Good chapter is 'After graduation. Will it all have been worthwhile?'

Tom Bourner and Phil Race (1990) *How to Win as a Part-Time Student: A Study Skills Guide*. London: Kogan Page. Concise, user-friendly, interactive. Each chapter threaded with SAQs (self analysis questions). Encourages an experiential process of review–do–reflect–revise.

Diane Collinson, Gillian Kirkup, Robin Kyd and Lynn Slocombe (1992) *Plain English* (2nd edn). Buckingham: Open University Press. Designed to meet the needs of all students who wish to improve their writing skills. Introductory quiz followed by sections on punctuation, spelling, grammar, style, references and bibliographies.

Gill Kirkup (1986) *Career-wise: A Fresh Start in Technology – Women Tell Their Stories*. Milton Keynes: Open University. Nine short biographies of women in their thirties and forties who began their OU studies as mature students and developed new careers in technology such as systems analyst, software manager, human factors engineer and computer programmer. Free from WISE, MK7 6AA.

Margaret Korving (1988) *Make a Fresh Start*. London: Kogan Page. Up-to-date, nationwide guide to hundreds of full-time, part-time and distance learning courses for women who want to start a new career, learn new skills, get new qualifications, develop new interests. Korving lists five types of courses for six areas of the UK, from London and Middlesex to Scotland and Northern Ireland. The category most relevant for people who lack academic self-confidence is called 'Pre-Entry, Sample and Access Courses'.

Margaret Korving (1989) *Training for Your Next Career*. London: Rosters Ltd. Rundown on ways to get more education as a mature adult and how to change careers mid-stream. Chapters on government schemes, employers' training schemes, professional courses, technical and commercial courses, independent colleges and distance learning.

National Extension College, 18 Brooklands Avenue, Cambridge CB2 2HN. Offers preparatory courses for the OU.

National Institute for Adult and Continuing Education, 19B de Montfort Street, Leicester LE1 7GE. Free leaflet, *Learning When You Are Older*.

Andy Northedge and others. *Living in a Changing Society*. Six modules for people thinking about taking up study for a degree. Module contains text and audio cassette. Milton Keynes: OU Educational Enterprises Ltd.

Andy Northedge (1990) *The Good Study Guide*. Milton Keynes: OU Educational Enterprises Ltd. Practical exercises, real-life examples and good advice enable students to develop effective

144

approaches to suit their individual learning styles and circumstances. Both an introductory workbook and highly useable reference book.

The Open College, Freepost TK1006, Brentford, Middlesex TW8 8BR. Short courses in a range of subjects such as accountancy, management, information technology and retailing.

The Open Learning Foundation, 24 Angel Gate, City Road, London EC1V 2RS. Has details of courses and contacts at 22 universities which support open learning.

Phil Race (1989) *The Open Learning Handbook*. London: Kogan Page. A first book for returners. All about writing essays, tutors, TMAs, CMAs and how to organize yourself to succeed at open learning.

Teresa Rickards (1992) *How to Win as a Mature Student*. London: Kogan Page. Self-help resource book of 20 units in 5 stages: Starting Out; Moving In; Acquiring Skills; Keeping Moving; Moving On.

Derek Rowntree (1991) *Teaching Yourself with Open Learning*. London: Sphere Books. A first book for returners. Chapters deal with: What can open learning offer you? How does open learning work? Getting organized. How to get help from other people. Are you getting value for money?

Judith Steiner (1989) *How to Survive as a Working Mother*. London: Kogan Page. How to balance a successful working life with bringing up a family.

Taking Liberties Collective (1989) *Learning the Hard Way: Women's Oppression in Men's Education*. London: Macmillan Education. The women of Southampton Women's Education Centre's 'Second Chance for Women' course tell the truth about their lives. Fifty-seven working-class women contributed to chapters with titles like 'The Obstacle Race' and 'Doing It for Ourselves'.

Women Returners' Network. Set up in 1984 to facilitate women's re-entry into the labour force by promoting education and training opportunities. Contact Margaret Johnson, WRN Secretary, Garden Cottage, Youngsbury, Ware, Herts SG12 0TZ.

Women Returners' Network (1992) *Returning to Work* (6th edn). London: Kogan Page. A directory of education and training for women. 1,500 courses in England, Northern Ireland, Scotland and Wales. List includes career-break, retainer and re-entry schemes, residential colleges for adults, childcare information.

Women Returners' Scheme Project, The Open University, Yorkshire Regional Centre, Fairfax House, Merrion Street, Leeds LS2 8JU. A year of part-time technical study for women at home who have technological backgrounds and previous work experience. Sponsored by High Technology National Training (HTNT).

Index